Classic
FRENCH
COOKING

Classic
FRENCH
COOKING

Recipes for mastering the French kitchen

ELISABETH LUARD

MQP

Published by **MQ Publications Limited**

12 The Ivories, 6–8 Northampton Street

London N1 2HY

Tel: 44 (0)20 7359 2244

Fax: 44 (0)20 7359 1616

email: mail@mqpublications.com

website: www.mqpublications.com

ISBN: 1-84072-724-1

3 5 7 9 0 8 6 4 2

Printed and bound in China

contents

introduction

The French know what they like and they know what they do well – in art, in philosophy and, above all, in the kitchen.

The recipes that define the everyday cooking of France – pâté de campagne, moules mariniére, steak au poivre, petits pois à la française, ratatouille, daube de bœuf, civet de liévre, lapin à la moutarde, gigot à l'ail, poulet à la crème, coq au vin, tarte au citron, mousse au chocolat – these are the recipes that need no translation, the ones that appear on every menu from Calais to Marseilles.

Fashions in food change – Thai today, Sicilian tomorrow – but whenever two or three food-lovers are gathered together to share a forkful of something special, France sets the standard by which all others are judged. No other tradition is as diverse, as vigorous or as capable of reinventing itself.

Happily for my infant tastebuds – endangered in youth by English boarding-school catering – I acquired my kitchen habits from a Frenchwoman, the formidable Bernadette, a cook employed by my stylish Jewish American grandmother. At the time, the early fifties, my grandmother had made

the Atlantic crossing, established herself in a large house in fashionable Belgrave Square and begun the assault on London society that was the duty of every American heiress. Born in Baltimore, heiress to a large British tobacco fortune, she was married at fifteen to a gambler (her cousin, the undoing of the family finances). Hers was a glamorous lifestyle. My grandfather gambled with King Farouk and played cards with Onassis. She was a friend of the Rothschilds and the Duchess of Windsor, whose lifestyle and tastes she shared, and the exquisite French food served at her table in defiance of post-war rationing turned her into one of London's most fashionable hostesses.

Although the staff who bustled about in the cavernous subterranean kitchens included a pastry-chef and a sauce chef – maître-saucier – as well as the usual complement of underlings, it was Bernadette who really ran the show. Bernadette who conducted the daily interview with my grandmother to determine the day's menu. Bernadette who dictated what came in and what went out of the kitchen. Bernadette who badgered the butcher, bullied the fishmonger and picked over every vegetable the greengrocer delivered. Bernadette shopped daily in Soho, bought nothing out of season and never let anything go to waste even though, as she was fond of lamenting, it was hard to find a reliable pork-butcher who might be trusted to feed the household's edible debris to a suitable pig. The shortages of post-war London did not make her any less demanding: she would rail against the impurity of the butter, the blandness of the cream, the unsuitability of British beef to dishes which demanded French veal.

She also ensured that I, the only granddaughter, already captivated by what went on in the kitchen, should acquire the basics of what, in her view, every young girl should know. This included how to tell the exact degree of doneness of a grilled entrecôte by testing it with your thumb; how to stop a béchamel from going lumpy by ensuring the liquid added was always boiling; how to judge the precise moment at which an omelette should be tipped out of the pan in order that it should be served baveuse – frothy within, firm without. Bernadette cooked instinctively, with the certainty of those who understand exactly why and what they do. And when my arm ached from beating the butter and sugar that went into her quatre-quarts – the French version of the English pound cake – she wouldn't let me set the bowl down until she had herself decided the mixture had achieved an acceptable lightness. She wrote nothing down and never ever, as far as I was aware, consulted a book or made a list. Looking back, it is quite possible she could neither read nor write; but she could cook and run a kitchen. My grandmother had to pay her more than any chef, though she told me this in the strictest confidence – as a matter of pride, she explained, rather than greed.

Happily, I was allowed to spend as much time in Bernadette's kingdom as I pleased. And pleasure – not perfection, not even the exact reproduction of a recipe – was what she sought to give. She had little respect for written recipes, dismissing them as largely unworkable, and saw no point in expensive ingredients if they did not, in her view, add to the enjoyment of what she cooked. She would cheerfully alter any recipe to suit the ingredients she had to hand. Her only rule was that if the ingredient was good when it came into the kitchen, all you had to do was not spoil it.

Later, as a teenager, I would join my grandmother in the various fashionable watering places where my grandfather played the tables. Monte Carlo, Montecatini, Eugénie les Bains, Marienbad, Deauville and Paris were all places where the rich and idle gathered to take the cure and the casinos made their profits. And since the main amusement was eating and drinking, these were the places to which the most ambitious young chefs were drawn. Cuisine minceur – later to develop into nouvelle cuisine – were inventions of the innovative chefs who catered to the overindulged and overweight in the spa-hotels. It was here, during the school holidays, I added further strands of experience to Bernadette's lessons. The chefs catering to the new body-conscious clients, such as my grandmother, were all young, eager and experimenting with new techniques, particularly the development of a new and lighter style of haute cuisine which appealed to the fashionable who were anxious to retain their figures.

When I married and had a family of my own, I added another level to my experience when I took us all (four children and husband) to live for one school year in the hinterland of Castelnaudary in the Languedoc – la France profonde, deepest France – so the children might have some experience of the French attitude to the good things of life. Living in an isolated farmhouse among a rural community whose way of life was still, in the seventies, as close to self-sufficiency as might be found anywhere in Europe, we had no choice but to follow the example of our neighbours and eat as the locals ate, acquiring along the way an understanding of peasant cookery – cuisine paysanne, the cooking of what comes to hand.

The great Curnonsky – gourmet, critic, boulevardier of the Belle Epoque, friend of Marcel Proust, author of the 32-volume *La France Gastronomique* and acknowledged father of modern French gastronomy – defined three interlinked traditions as crucial to the identification of a national culinary habit. The first, he explained, is haute cuisine, the grand gastronomy of the court. The second, cuisine bourgeois, the cooking of the citizens of the towns who had access to all good things. The third – some would say the most valuable – is peasant cookery, the culinary habit of those who cook and eat what they grow, harvest and gather for themselves. Only by considering all three of these strands, he concluded, can the excellence of the national cuisine be measured. And France, he observed, excels in all three.

France, as an affiliation of kingdoms, duchies and counties of relatively recent date (a mere five centuries or so), has always been resolutely regional. Beyond the obvious divisions (such as the region's preferred frying-medium: olive oil in the south, goose fat in the middle, butter in the north) a nation capable of appreciating five hundred different cheeses is scarcely likely to be willing to sacrifice diversity to mass-production, whether of ingredients or culinary habit. Allegiances are to locality – city, village, valley, community – and regional dishes reflect what is grown, gathered or husbanded in the area, a culinary style known as cuisine du terroir, the cooking of the terrain. Visitors looking for French food in a French town, accustomed in their home-territory to a wide choice of culinary styles, are often startled when they find the same menu posted outside every restaurant of the region. The exceptions to this are cosmopolitan cities such as Paris – which, as the capital, had no need to develop a particular culinary style since everyone else's was readily available.

Cuisine du terroir makes the choucroute of Alsace as different from the garbures of Gascogny as the pissaladière of Provence from the moules marinières of Brittany.

The French have never been squeamish about what they eat, still less about the form in which they buy it. Offal, both fresh and in the form of tripe-sausages, is eaten without inhibition. Feet and heads are left on poultry so that the purchaser can identify the breed as well as appreciate the freshness. Anyone who lives within reach of the sea expects to buy fish straight from the net: at least one boat of any inshore fleet sells its catch direct to the customers. In the fishmonger, the catch is displayed in the round – with scales, heads and innards still in place – and is prepared at the request of the purchaser. Shellfish and crustaceans are sold live in the confident expectation that the purchaser will know what to do with them.

If he or she wants something ready prepared, the French cook goes to the traiteur, the cooked-food shop, and cheerfully admits as much, recommending the place to friends. The traiteur, too, provides the little hors d'œuvres without which no French repast is worthy of the name: rillettes, olives, pâtés, charcuterie, the classic salads (potato, carrot, celeriac). Desserts are rarely prepared at home; meals usually end with cheese and fruit. If something special is called for, the best pâtisserie in town is alerted and the dessert ordered in advance – shop-bought tarts have glamour, as does the Twelfth Night pithiviers or the

Christmas bûche de noël. And then there's the crowning glory, the weekly visit to the cheese-merchant for a slice of Roquefort, a slab of Cantal, a soft-hearted Camembert, a few little rounds of blue-bloomed goat's-milk cheese.

In France, all these good things are considered an indivisible part of the joy of life: of the French it can truly be said that they live to eat. Whether they do this in Michelin-starred restaurants (the natural heirs of court cuisine); or allow the traiteur to take most of the strain (one of the pleasures of the town-based bourgeoisie); or take the rural way and cook whatever's in season right now. In France, the produce of small-holding self-sufficiency, while no longer a matter of necessity, remains a choice, even for those who rely on others to bring it to market.

Of the thousands of recipes which have fair claim to inclusion in a book on the classic cooking of France, I have chosen nearer a hundred. The task was not easy. In the end it came down to a simple matter of personal choice. I have included those recipes that I consider essential to pass on to my own grandchildren, just as Bernadette passed hers on to me.

Bon appétit.

hors d'œuvres

tapenade

BLACK OLIVE *and* ANCHOVY PASTE

The tapenade, surprisingly, is a relatively new introduction to the hors d'œuvre repertoire. A restaurant invention from the Cote d'Azure, it takes its name from the capers – tapeno in the Provençale patois – that perfume the mix. Nevertheless, the idea of pitting and pounding olives to make a savoury paste to eat with bread is nothing new, it's just the sophisticated blending with other storecupboard ingredients that makes the difference. For the basic olive paste, choose the wrinkled, ripe, chewy little frost-cured olives of Nyons or anywhere in Upper Provence.

Makes about 500g (1lb 2oz)

250g (9oz) black Provençal olives
6 preserved anchovy fillets
1 tablespoon preserved tuna
2 tablespoons preserved capers
1 teaspoon freshly milled black pepper
1 teaspoon dried thyme
about 120ml (4fl oz) olive oil
1 teaspoon brandy

1 Drain the olives and remove the stones. Drain the anchovy fillets. Salted anchovy fillets from a barrel have to be soaked in milk for 30 minutes and then boned.

2 Pound all the solid ingredients together to a fine paste in a mortar. Trickle in enough olive oil to make a smooth scoopable paste, beating with a wooden spoon as for a mayonnaise. Stir in the brandy. Alternatively, save your strength and puree the whole lot in a food processor.

3 To store the tapenade, pot it, cover with a tight-fitting lid and keep in the fridge.

SERVING SUGGESTION ~ Serve with chunks of baguette and red radishes. In France, radishes are sold with their leaves, with the stalks bunched into a posy, and this is how they appear on the table.

USING TAPENADE ~ Tapenade can be used as a stuffing for hard-boiled eggs. Shell and halve the eggs lengthwise. Remove the yolks and mash with 1 teaspoon tapenade per yolk. Spoon or pipe the mixture back into the whites.

brandade de morue

T his is the dish traditionally served in Provence and the Languedoc at the souper maigre, the fasting supper of Christmas Eve, at which neither meat, wine nor sweet things can be served. You can buy morue, salt cod, pre-soaked and ready to go; if not, choose a middle cut and soak it for 48 hours in several changes of water.

Serves 6–8

500g (1lb 2oz) salt cod, pre-soaked
1 onion, cut into chunks
2 bay leaves
2–3 fennel tops or 1 teaspoon fennel seeds
1 teaspoon white peppercorns
300ml (½ pint) extra virgin olive oil, warmed to finger-heat
2–3 tablespoons cream, warmed
1 potato, boiled, mashed and still warm
(optional, but it helps the emulsion)
2–3 garlic cloves, crushed
1 black olive

TO SERVE
melba toast
(fine slices of dry bread toasted in the oven until crisp)

1 Cut the fish into 3–4 chunks and put these in a saucepan with the onion, bay leaves, fennel tops or seeds and peppercorns. Cover with water and bring gently to the boil.

2 Remove the pan from the heat as soon as the water gives a good belch, and pour in a glassful of cold water. Leave to stand for 5 minutes. Then drain, skin and flake the fish, discarding any bones.

3 Pound the flaked fish with the potato (if using), the garlic and a little of the oil, and then mash thoroughly and vigorously. Beat in the rest of the oil gradually, as if making a mayonnaise, adding the cream towards the end. Beat the mixture to a thick, scoopable white puree. You can also do this in a food processor, but the result will be noticeably smoother and whiter than that achieved by hand-beating.

4 Pile the mixture into a bowl and top with a single black olive. Serve at room temperature with melba toast.

rillettes

POTTED PORK

*N*either a pâté nor a paste, but something in between,
you'll find this succulent preparation on sale in
charcuteries and pork-butchers throughout France, prepared to
a recipe scarcely changed since the days of Charlemagne. The
lard which serves as the potting agent for the meat is either
goose fat, made with the rich leavings from the foie-gras goose,
or panne de porc, the soft white fat that surrounds a pig's
kidney. Serve rillettes with fresh radishes, pickles, unsalted
butter, rough salt (preferably sel de Guerande) and chunks of
fresh baguette or pain de campagne – country bread, the name
given to a round loaf suitable for carrying in the pocket.
Rillettes may also be served as part of a selection of charcuterie:
jambon de bayonne, saucisson sec, andouillette.

Serves 8–10

175g (6oz) goose fat or freshly made pork lard
1.5kg (3¼lb) belly pork, skinned and cut into chunks
3 teaspoons salt
1 teaspoon freshly milled pepper
1 teaspoon ground allspice
a small bunch of thyme, rosemary and bay

1 Melt the lard gently in a heavy pan without letting it bubble. Add the pork and stir over a very low heat until the fat begins to run from the meat.

2 Add 1 tablespoon water, the salt, pepper and allspice. Tuck in the herbs between the pieces of meat and cook very gently for 3 hours until the fat has completely melted and the meat is absolutely soft. Alternatively, bake in the coolest possible oven, at 75°C (167°F). Keep a careful watch for sticking, stirring the pork regularly. The fat should never bubble and the temperature must remain very low throughout cooking. At the end, there should be no water and the fat should be clear and the meat meltingly soft.

3 Remove the herbs. Skim off and save a ladleful of the surface fat for sealing the pots. Then using two forks, pull the meat apart, mixing it with the fat until well blended or pound it in a mortar (or use a food processor sparingly) to make a smoother mix. Taste and adjust the seasoning.

4 Pot the rillettes in small sterilized jars and leave to cool. Pour in a layer of the reserved melted fat to seal. The rillettes are ready immediately or will keep, undisturbed, for up to a month in the fridge or almost indefinitely in the freezer.

PREPARING PORK LARD ~ When preparing pork lard, take care to strip the little fat globules from the membranes and melt it very slowly with enough water to prevent it from browning.

pâté de campagne

COUNTRY PÂTÉ

A pâté, strictly speaking, is a pie, a description that indicates a pie crust; however, such refinements do not apply in the rural kitchen, where a jacket of finely sliced salt-cured belly pork – petit salé – or bacon serves to keep the mixture moist, the main purpose of the crust. You can replace the lean pork with the same volume of chicken or game, but do not omit the fat pork as wild meat needs something rich and fatty to balance its natural dryness.

Serves 6–8

1kg (2¼lb) boneless lean pork shoulder, cubed
225g (8oz) belly pork, skinned and cubed
1 tablespoon white brandy or Calvados (optional)
1 garlic clove, coarsely crushed
1 teaspoon dried thyme
1 teaspoon dried rosemary
1 teaspoon juniper berries, crushed
1 egg
100ml (3½fl oz) dry white wine
1 teaspoon ground allspice
1 teaspoon salt
1 teaspoon crushed black peppercorns
2 tablespoons fresh breadcrumbs
about 10 thin slices petit salé (salt-cured belly pork) or streaky bacon
2–3 bay leaves

1 For a gamey flavour, start the day before and marinate the pork overnight: place both types in a dish with the brandy or calvados (if using), garlic, thyme, rosemary and juniper.

2 Preheat the oven to 180°C (350°F, gas 4). Drain the meat reserving all the marinade. Chop half the pork shoulder and half the belly pork either using a sharp knife or briefly in a food processor. Mince the remainder. Place all the meat in a bowl.

3 Fork the egg with the wine and pour over the meat. Add the reserved marinade, allspice, salt and peppercorns. Work the ingredients well with the meat and then mix in the breadcrumbs.

4 Line a 500g (1lb 2oz) loaf tin with petit salé or bacon, leaving the ends overlapping the rim to fold over the top. Pack in the meat – the mixture should about two-thirds fill the tin. Top with the bay leaves and fold over the lining.

5 Cut a piece of foil large enough to cover the tin and pleat it down the middle to allow room for expansion. Cover the tin with this foil and set it in a bain-marie, a roasting tin into which you have poured enough boiling water to come half way up the sides of the loaf tin.

6 Bake for about 1 hour, until the pâté is perfectly firm and well-shrunk from the sides of the tin. Test with a skewer thrust deep into the middle: the juices should run clear. Leave to cool. Cover with a clean cloth and set a weighted board on top. Leave to rest and firm up overnight – this is important or the pâté will not hold together.

SERVING SUGGESTIONS ~ Serve with a bunch of little rosy radishes, black olives (or a tapenade, see page 16/17, the more elegant alternative), and chunks of freshly baked baguette – a pâté without bread is unthinkable.

French pork-butchery, traditionally a specialist business reflecting the importance of the pig in the life of rural households, is an art as well as a craft. Pork-butchers take pride in preparing their own charcuterie, a definition applied to pork-products of a lightly preserved kind as well as the more durable (and familiar) air-cured hams and slicing-sausages. The repertoire evolved commercially to take care of the less saleable bits – innards and those parts which are too fatty or bony or troublesome to prepare – but was, in essence, a response to the need to add shelf-life to perishable foodstuffs in the days when refrigeration was not an option. Any self-respecting pork-butcher on market-day will be able to offer half a dozen freshly-cooked pâtés both rough and smooth; a choice of rillettes and rillons – shredded pork conserved in lard, petit salé – salt-cured belly pork – useful for enriching bean-dishes as well as, thinly sliced, for lining the pâté-tin or protecting the breast of a bird from the heat of the oven. There will, too, be trotters ready-cooked, boned and breadcrumbed for grilling, head-cheese set in its own jelly, pork-knuckles and bits to strengthen the pot-au-feu. For those who appreciate blood-puddings there'll be boudin noir as well as the creamy, more delicate boudin blanc; for those who love innards, there'll be the peppery tripe-sausages – andouille and andouillettes – tightly rolled into bolsters for grilling, delicious with strong French mustard. The French housewife takes pride in her choice of charcutier, values what he does and wouldn't dream of pretending she'd made something herself if she hadn't. Being prepared to pay for the butcher's expertise is part of the pleasure.

pâté de foie de porc

PORK LIVER PÂTÉ

This is an honest country recipe for ensuring that the more perishable products of the rural household's annual pig-slaughter did not go to waste – a responsibility now transferred to the pork-butcher.

Serves 4–6

1 tablespoon pork lard or butter
500g (1lb 2oz) pork liver, cut into strips
2 shallots or 1 small onion, finely chopped
250g (9oz) lean pork shoulder
250g (9oz) belly pork
1 egg
1 teaspoon dried thyme
½ teaspoon juniper berries, crushed
½ teaspoon grated nutmeg
¼ teaspoon ground cloves
8–10 thin slices streaky bacon or salt-cured
belly pork (petit salé)
salt and freshly milled pepper
2 bay leaves

TO SERVE
radishes/pickled cucumbers
baguette/unsalted butter

1 Melt the butter or lard in a frying pan. Add the liver and onion and turn the ingredients in the butter until the meat stiffens, but is still pink. Remove from the heat.

2 Preheat the oven to 180°C (350°F, gas 4). Mince the shoulder and belly pork together. Chop or mince the contents of the pan with the minced pork. Transfer to a bowl. Using your hands, work in the egg, thyme, juniper, nutmeg and cloves. Season with salt and pepper.

3 Line a 500g (1lb 2oz) loaf tin with slices of salt pork or bacon, reserving some for the top. Pack in the meat mixture. Place the bay leaves on top and cover with bacon rashers. Set the tin in a bain-marie, a roasting tin into which you have poured enough boiling water to come half way up the sides of the loaf tin.

4 Bake for about 1 hour, until the top browns a little. Cover with foil and continue baking for another 30 minutes, until the juices run clear when a skewer is pushed into the middle.

5 Place a weight on top of the pâté and leave it to cool, preferably overnight. The pâté will keep for 2 weeks in the fridge.

6 Serve thickly sliced, with radishes, pickled cucumbers, fresh baguette and unsalted butter.

confit de foie gras

POTTED GOOSE LIVER

The goose and the duck are both candidates for engorgeage, a process by which the birds are force fed until their livers are very enlarged and full of fat. Maize is the usual fodder, chestnuts and walnuts traditional. This condition is not entirely unnatural as it was recorded in Egypt during the time of the Pharoahs, when the livers of migrant geese that had stuffed themselves on the young grasses on the floodplain of the Nile were so swollen they prevented the birds from becoming airborn. Toulouse, Périgueux and Strasbourg are the main centres of foie-gras production in France. In truffle-producing areas, such as the Périgord, slivers of the fresh tuber – in season at the same time as the goose – are included.

Serves 8–10

1 fresh foie gras weighing 1–1.5kg (2¼–3¼ lb)
1–2 tablespoons coarse salt
1 tablespoon Armagnac or white brandy (optional)
1 fresh black Perigord truffle, brushed and
cut into slivers (optional)
250g (9oz) pure white goose or duck fat
pain de levain (country sour-dough bread) to serve

1 Remove any veins from the foie gras. Check the thick end of each lobe for the main vein; once found, tug it gently to expose its full length as well as the subsidiary veins, and remove them carefully with a small sharp knife. Remove any dark blood vessels. Do not worry about making a mess of the liver as it will re-form as it cooks. Place the liver on a clean china plate and sprinkle it all over with the salt and the Armagnac or brandy (if using). Cover with another clean plate and weight it down. Leave overnight to drain.

2 Preheat the oven to 190°C (375°F, gas 5). Drain off the juices, dust off excess salt and pat the liver dry. If using truffle, make little slits in the liver and push the truffle slivers into them. Weigh the liver and calculate the cooking time at 20 minutes per 500g (1lb 2oz). Pack the liver into a terrine that will just accommodate it. Ladle in enough melted goose fat to submerge the liver completely.

3 Cover with foil, shiny side down, and transfer to a bain-marie, a roasting tin into which you have poured enough boiling water to come half way up the sides of the terrine. Bake for the calculated time, until the juices run clear but are still pale pink when the liver is pierced with a sharp skewer. Allow to cool. Serve country-style with toasted sour-dough bread, pain de levain.

SELECTING FOIE GRAS ~ To choose foie, look for firmness and paleness – ivory lightly tinged with pink (Strasbourg foie is naturally pinker). A yellow tint is a sign, along with excessive size, that the liver will be overly fatty. There should also be no sign of green staining, an indication of a punctured gall bladder which, if allowed to seep into the liver, turns the whole liver bitter.

escargots à la bourguignonne

VINEYARD SNAILS *with* GARLIC BUTTER

All snails, of whatever size or breed, are edible. Our ancestors loved them: stone-age middens are full of the debris of snail-feasts. The only danger lies not in the meat itself, but in what the creature might have ingested. Its digestive system is capable of processing the most toxic substances and depositing them in the cloaca, the little dark curl of intestine at the end of the body. Toxicity can be removed either by a period of starvation or hibernation, or control of the diet by other means (migrating the snails to the vineyard), or by removing the meat from the shell and pinching off the cloaca after a short (5 minute) plunge in the boiling-pot. After this, a gentle simmer with aromatics and wine will improve the flavour while tenderising the meat; this preliminary will have been carried out if you buy snails ready-prepared for finishing. In France two varieties are eaten. The smaller of the two is the petit gris, a snail with a soft grey body and a brown shell marked with a feathery pattern; the other is the larger Burgundy, or vineyard, snail. Both are endangered in the wild and are largely replaced with imported snails from Turkey and the Far East. For this dish, you need the larger snails. Allow six to twelve ready-prepared snails with their shells per person.

48 ready-prepared snails with shells
2–3 tablespoons Pernod (optional)

GARLIC BUTTER
250g (9oz) unsalted butter, softened
2 garlic cloves, crushed
1 tablespoon finely chopped shallot
2 tablespoons finely chopped flat-leaf parsley
salt and freshly milled pepper

TO SERVE
fresh baguette

1 Preheat the oven to 180°C (350°F, gas 4). Arrange the empty snail shells, mouths pointing upwards, in special snail platters or in a roasting tin on a bed of rough salt (dishwasher salt is fine). Pop a drop of Pernod (if using) into each shell.

2 Mash the ingredients for the garlic butter together until well blended, seasoning with a little salt and plenty of freshly milled pepper. Drop a little butter into the base of a shell, top with the snail meat and close the shell with another knob of butter. Replace the shell in the container, mouth still pointing upwards. Continue until all are filled.

3 Bake the snails for 20–30 minutes, until steaming hot and bubbling. Serve with chunks of fresh baguette for mopping up the butter.

cassolette d'escargots

SNAIL CASSEROLE

*T*his is a sophisticated Provençal recipe for France's mighty mollusks. Snails in garlic-butter is all very well in dairy-country, but in the land of the olive tree where dairy foods are traditionally absent, oil is the enrichment of choice.

Serves 6

2 glasses white wine
500g (1lb 2oz) shelled cooked snails
(cooking broth reserved, see page 30)
2 tablespoons olive oil
1 tablespoon plain flour
2 tablespoons grated cheese, such as Cantal or Gruyère
salt and freshly milled pepper
pinch of sugar (optional)
2–3 sage leaves, finely chopped
2 tablespoons chopped parsley
2 tablespoons snipped chives

TO FINISH
2 heaped tablespoons fresh breadcrumbs
2 tablespoons chopped parsley
1 garlic clove, finely chopped
2 tablespoons grated cheese
1 tablespoon olive oil

1 Bring the wine to the boil in a saucepan with a ladleful of the snail broth (see page 30) or any decent stock and cook until the liquid is reduced by half.

2 Work the oil with the flour to a paste, then whisk it into the reduced broth. Simmer until thick enough to coat the back of a wooden spoon. Stir in the grated cheese. Taste and add salt and pepper – maybe a pinch of sugar it the wine was a little tart.

3 Add the snails and simmer gently for 10 minutes to marry the flavours. Stir in the chopped herbs.

4 To finish, preheat the grill. Spread the snails in a gratin dish. Toss the breadcrumbs with the parsley, garlic and grated cheese, and sprinkle over the snails. Drizzle with the olive oil and flash under the grill to gild the top. If the snails are prepared in advance ready for finishing, preheat the oven to 180°C (350°F, gas 4) and bake for 15 minutes to bubble and brown.

cuisses de grenouille à l'ail

FROGS' LEGS *with* GARLIC AND PARSLEY

Frogs' legs were readily available from the wild some thirty years ago, when my children attended school in Castelnaudary in the Languedoc. We lived in a farmhouse surrounded by fields, copses and ponds where frogs could be caught by attaching a scrap of red rag to a fishing line. Frogs can no longer be legally caught in the wild and France's supplies of muscular little frogs' legs – they always come in pairs – are mostly imported from the paddy fields of South East Asia. Possible substitutes are quails' legs – once cooked they look much the same (sauté the breasts with mushrooms).

Serves 4–6

8–12 pairs frogs' legs
1–2 tablespoons plain flour, seasoned
4 tablespoons olive oil
50g (2oz) unsalted butter
4 garlic cloves, finely chopped
2 tablespoons chopped parsley
squeeze of lemon juice

TO SERVE
quartered lemons
fresh baguette

1 Dust the frogs' legs lightly with the seasoned flour.

2 Heat the oil in a heavy frying pan. Add the butter and wait until it froths. Lower the heat a little, lay the frogs' legs gently in the pan and sauté for 2–3 minutes on each side, until they take a little colour and the meat feels firm when pressed with your thumb.

3 Transfer to a warm serving dish. Add the garlic to the pan drippings and fry for a couple of minutes until the garlic softens, then stir in the parsley and add a squeeze of lemon.

4 Return the frogs' legs to the pan and reheat gently. Serve with quartered lemons and chunks of very fresh baguette.

galantine de gibier

GAME TERRINE *with* JELLY

Y ou never can tell what the hunters will bring home. A galantine – the French method of potting by slow cooking with aromatics in just enough water to cover the meats – is the practical way to deal with a mixed bag of furred and feathered beasts of uncertain age and toughness. If you lack a good proportion of bone to meat, include a well-scrubbed pig's trotter or a piece of veal shin to help the juices set to a firm jelly. This popular dish is sold sliced by weight from the traiteur, the cooked-food shop. It is good with a few salt-pickled caper buds and baby cucumbers (cornichons) to cut the richness, or serve it with a salad and new potatoes as a light supper.

Serves 8–10

**2–3kg (4½–6½lb) wild boar or any game on the bone, chopped
into manageable chunks or portions
2–3 thyme sprigs
2–3 bay leaves
1 tablespoon juniper berries, crushed
1 tablespoon salt
1 teaspoon crushed black peppercorns
1 tablespoon Calvados or white brandy
4–5 thin slices bayonne ham**

1 Preheat the oven to 160°C (325°F, gas 3). Pack the meat, bones and all, into a large casserole or stone crock with the thyme, bay leaves, juniper berries, salt and peppercorns. Pour in the Calvados or brandy and enough water to cover the meat.

2 Cover with a lid that fits very tightly. (Seal the rim with a flour-and-water paste if the lid does not fit really snugly.) Cook for 3–4 hours, until the meat is really soft.

3 Remove the meat and strain the broth. While the meat is still warm, strip it off the bones, and dice it. The broth needs to be really strong if it is to set properly in a jelly: boil it until it is reduced to about 450ml (¾ pint).

4 Line a 1kg (2¼lb) loaf tin with the ham, leaving generous flaps overhanging the rim. Pack in the meat mixture, filling the tin right to the top. Pour in enough of the concentrated stock to wet the meat thoroughly. Fold the loose flaps of ham over the top, cover with foil and weight down. Leave the tin in a cool place overnight for the jelly to set. To serve, use a knife dipped in boiling water to cut the meat in slices.

STORING THE GALANTINE ~ The galantine keeps well in the fridge, but it does not freeze. The jelly will separate and there'll be no hope for the galantine, other than to boil it again and bake it in a pie.

terrine de legumes

VEGETABLE TERRINE

This is a useful starter for vegetarians as the French hors
d'œuvre table tends to be meat orientated. The choice of
vegetables is up to you, though these look particularly pretty
and the flavours are well balanced.

Serves 6–8

500g (1lb 2oz) spinach or broccoli
500g (1lb 2oz) celeriac or cauliflower
500g (1lb 2oz) carrots or swede
3 large eggs
300ml (½ pint) single cream
¼ teaspoon freshly grated nutmeg
salt and freshly milled pepper

1 If using spinach, wash it and then place in a lidded pan with the water that clings to the leaves. Cook briefly until wilted and drain thoroughly, squeezing out the water by hand. Cut the other vegetables into bite-sized pieces and cook each type separately in boiling salted water until soft. Drain thoroughly, and puree the vegetables, still keeping them separate.

2 Preheat the oven to 150°C (300°F, gas 2). Butter a 500g (1lb 2oz) loaf tin. Separate the eggs. Mix the yolks thoroughly into the cream. Whisk the whites until fluffy, smooth and light. Mix a third of the yolk and cream mixture into each vegetable puree. Season carefully before folding in the whites, equally divided among the three mixtures.

3 Spread the purees in layers in the prepared tin, first spinach, then celeriac, then carrot. Cover with foil, shiny side down, and set the tin in a bain-marie, a roasting tin into which you have poured enough boiling water to come half way up the sides of the loaf tin. Bake for 1½ hours, until perfectly set – test by pressing with your finger. Allow to cool and become firm.

4 When you are ready to serve the terrine, unmould it on to a plate. Serve at room temperature, cut into beautiful three-coloured slices.

SERVING TIP ~ The terrine is good with a chilled sauce, maybe crème fraîche blended with finely chopped watercress or chives, or a fresh tomato coulis (see page 255).

pissaladière

PROVENÇALE ONION TART

This speciality of the bakers of Nice is a close relation of the Italian pizza – some might say the original of the genre, since it gets its name from the pissalat niçoise, a paste made by pounding salt-cured anchovies with olive oil, thyme, pepper and bay. In its simplest form, the base is a thin bread dough topped by a thick layer of softly-fried onion.

Serves 6–8

225g (8oz) plain flour
½ teaspoon salt
3 tablespoons olive oil
1 egg
½ teaspoon finely grated lemon zest

TOPPING
1kg (2¼lb) onions, thinly sliced
1–2 tablespoons olive oil
2–3 garlic cloves, finely chopped
6–8 anchovy fillets
2 tablespoons black olives
2 tablespoons salt-cured capers, rinsed and drained
1 tablespoon chopped fresh thyme

1 Work the flour, salt, olive oil, egg and lemon zest together by hand, adding about 4 tablespoons warm water to form a soft, smooth ball of dough that leaves the sides of the bowl clean. (Alternatively, this may be done in a food processor.) Flatten the dough a little, cover it with cling film and set it aside to rest for 30 minutes.

2 Meanwhile, prepare the filling. Fry the onions gently in the oil until they soften and gild – don't hurry the process or let them burn.

3 Preheat the oven to 425°F (220°C, gas 7).Transfer the dough to a floured surface and roll it out to fit a large baking tray, about 25cm (10in) square. Spread the dough with the onions and top with the garlic, anchovies, olives, capers and thyme.

4 Bake for 20–25 minutes, until the pastry is crisp and golden, and the edges have blistered brown.

salade niçoise

SALAD NIÇOISE

A robust, chunky summer salad, this is served as a first course or a light lunch. Named after Nice, where the Italian culinary influence is strong, the flavouring herb is basil. Do not include cooked vegetables as the flavours should be fresh, bright and clean to contrast with the salty, fermented flavour of the preserved fish.

Serves 4

4 hard-boiled eggs
500g (1lb 2oz) ripe tomatoes
1 small cucumber
1 cos or romaine lettuce heart, roughly chopped
6 salted anchovies or anchovies canned in oil
150g (5oz) salted tuna in oil
1 garlic clove
6 tablespoons olive oil
2 tablespoons wine vinegar
1 green pepper, seeded and sliced into rings
4–5 spring onions, chopped
1 mild purple onion, cut vertically into thin slivers
handful of shelled young broad beans or baby green beans (raw)
1 tablespoon black olives
about 12 fresh basil leaves, roughly torn

1 Peel the eggs and quarter them neatly. Chop the tomatoes and cucumber into bite-sized chunks. Tear the lettuce into bite-sized pieces. Drain the anchovies and the tuna. Break the tuna into large flakes and separate the anchovies into fillets.

2 Rub the salad bowl with the cut clove of garlic. Pour the oil and vinegar into the bowl and use a fork to mix them. Toss the lettuce, tomatoes, cucumber, green pepper, spring onions, purple onion and beans with the oil and vinegar. Do not add salt – the fish and olives provide quite enough of their own.

3 Finish with the olives, basil leaves, eggs, tuna and anchovies.

HARD-BOILED EGGS ~ Bring the eggs to room temperature and place them in enough cold water to cover them completely and bring the water to the boil. After 3 minutes, remove the pan from the heat and leave the eggs to stand for 8–10 minutes, depending on their size. Plunge the eggs into cold water to loosen the shells, then peel them.

PREPARING SALTED ANCHOVIES ~ Salted anchovies from the barrel need to be soaked in milk for a few hours to make them less salty. Then they should be drained and de-whiskered by removing the hairy little bones – pinch them between the thumb and forefinger to loosen, then pull them out.

salade de pommes de terre

POTATO SALAD

*C*hoose one of the small, almond-shaped potato varieties
that remain firm after cooking, such as Charlotte or La
Ratte, France's salad potato of choice. Although the marjoram
included in the recipe is not essential, it has a warm earthy
fragrance that gives it a particularly affinity with potato.

Serves 4–6

1kg (2¼lb) small new potatoes, scrubbed
4 tablespoons olive oil
1–2 slices day-old bread, cut into cubes
1 garlic clove, crushed with a pinch of salt

DRESSING
2 tablespoons mild mustard (preferably Dijon mustard)
2 tablespoons wine vinegar
1 glass white wine or meat stock
4 tablespoons olive oil
salt and freshly milled pepper

TO FINISH
1 tablespoon capers, drained
1 tablespoon small black olives
small bunch of spring onions, trimmed and chopped
a few marjoram leaves to finish

1 Cook the potatoes in plenty of well-salted boiling water for 15–20 minutes, until perfectly tender. Drain immediately, then return the potatoes to the heat for a moment to dry them off.

2 Meanwhile, heat the oil in a frying pan. As soon as it smokes – a blue haze, nothing more – drop in the bread cubes and fry them until crisp and golden. Remove, toss with the crushed garlic and reserve.

3 Set the frying pan with its oily drippings back on the heat and stir in the mustard, vinegar and wine or stock. Bubble up for a moment and whisk in the oil and seasoning. If you're lucky, the dressing will form an emulsion; if not, no matter. Tip the dressing into the bowl in which you mean to serve the salad.

4 Slice the potatoes into the bowl, skin and all, and turn them in the hot liquid. Add the capers, olives and spring onions and turn them with the potatoes. The potatoes will drink it all up as they cool. Finish, when cool, with a few leaves of marjoram.

VARIATIONS ~ Other ingredients can be added to the potato salad. Possible inclusions are diced cucumber, hard-boiled egg, tomato, diced apple, walnuts, toasted pine kernels, preserved tuna or anchovies.

ratatouille

PROVENÇAL VEGETABLES IN OLIVE OIL

*T*his is a dish for high summer when the sunny vegetables
of Provence are at peak perfection. The aubergines
should be cut into dice about the size of a hazelnut (modern
varieties do not need salting); the courgettes should be
quartered if large and cut into slices as thick as your little
finger. Each element of the assembly is permitted to take the heat
separately and combined at the end – a little labour intensive
but essential if the dish is to be as good as it should be.

Serves 6

150ml (¼ pint) olive oil (possibly more)
2 aubergines, diced
2 red peppers, seeded and thinly sliced
1 green chilli, seeded and chopped (optional but good)
3–4 small courgettes, sliced
2–3 onions, finely sliced
4–5 garlic cloves
3–4 ripe plum tomatoes, peeled and diced
(bottled or canned are fine)
1½ teaspoons dried rosemary
1½ teaspoons dried thyme
salt and freshly milled pepper

1 Heat half the oil in a roomy frying pan. Add the aubergines, sprinkle with a little salt and fry gently until perfectly tender and lightly caramelised. The aubergines will first fry, then soak up the oil, and finally give it back and fry again.

2 Transfer the aubergines to a large sieve set over a bowl to catch the drippings. Reheat the pan with another 2 tablespoons oil and add the red peppers and the chilli (if using). Fry gently until the peppers are soft and lightly caramelised, then transfer them to the sieve.

3 Reheat the pan with another 2 tablespoons oil and fry the courgettes until soft and lightly gilded, then transfer to the sieve with the aubergines.

4 Return the drippings from the vegetables to the pan and fry the onions and garlic until soft and golden. Remove and drain in the sieve over the bowl. Reheat the pan with the remaining oil and any residual drippings and fry the tomatoes gently until soft and collapsed.

5 Stir in the rosemary and thyme, and the vegetables from the sieve. Season with salt and pepper, and bubble gently for 5–10 minutes to marry the flavours. Serve at room temperature.

NOTE ~ The only essential ingredients are the aubergines, garlic, onions and oil.

céleri-rave rémoulade

GRATED CELERIAC *with* MUSTARD VINAIGRETTE

A rémoulade is simply a mustard-thickened vinaigrette which often includes capers, chopped spring onion, hard-boiled egg and chopped herbs, and is used as a sharp little sauce for cold meats from the charcuterie. Here it is used as a dressing for grated raw celeriac. Lighter and sharper than a mayonnaise-dressed salad, celeriac salad can be bought ready-made in the traiteur by weight, where it is sold as one-third of a classic trio of salads. The other two salads are finely-grated raw carrot dressed with lemon juice, olive oil and black olives, and baked beetroot dressed with olive oil, garlic and parsley.

1 celeriac root
1 tablespoon mild Dijon mustard
6 tablespoons olive oil
1 tablespoon wine vinegar or cider vinegar
salt and freshly milled black pepper
chopped flat-leaf parsley (optional) to garnish

1 Peel the celeriac root, cut it into manageable chunks and grate it coarsely. (Use a food processor if you have the appropriate attachment.)

2 Add the celeriac to a large saucepan of boiling salted water and bring the water back to the boil – this should take about 3 minutes, just long enough to blanch the celeriac. Transfer the celeriac to a sieve or colander, pass it under the cold tap to stop the cooking process, and drain thoroughly.

3 To make the rémoulade: in a small bowl, work the mustard with the oil, whisking or forking the oil in drop by drop, as if making a mayonnaise. Add the vinegar as the sauce emulsifies. Taste and add salt and pepper.

4 Dress the celeriac with the rémoulade. Finish with a handful of parsley – or not, as you please.

asperges à la vinaigrette

ASPARAGUS *with* OIL AND VINEGAR

The French like blanched asparagus – fat and white with a cream-coloured tip – while the Germans like theirs blanched and tipped with violet, and the English (as well as the Spaniards) prefer theirs green. For the spears to remain perfectly blanched, they must be picked before dawn from beds well-heaped with sandy soil, so the tips which thrust upwards overnight have no chance to reach the light. The asparagus beds of southern France were planted as a replacement crop for the olive trees lost to the frost during the terrible winter of 1956. Although most of the crop is exported to northern markets, the locals appreciate theirs with no other sauce but the mild golden olive oil of Provence forked until blended with just enough vinegar to give it an edge.

Serves 4

1kg (2¼lb) large white asparagus
150ml (¼ pint) extra virgin olive oil
3 tablespoons wine vinegar
salt and freshly milled black pepper
fresh baguette

1 Have ready an asparagus steamer or a pan deep enough to accommodate the bundles of asparagus vertically; that is, with their heads in the air and the stalks in water. (You can improvise a steamer by cutting the top off of an empty 5-litre olive oil can.)

2 Wash and trim the asparagus stalks and tie them into neat bundles. Bring a large pan of salted water to a rolling boil and lower the bundles in, feet first. Prop them up so that the stalks are submerged but the tips are in steam only. Bring the water back to the boil, turn the heat down, and boil gently for 15–20 minutes, until the stalks are soft.

3 Meanwhile, prepare a jug of the olive oil forked up with the wine vinegar – leave the fork in the jug so that oil and vinegar can be blended again.

4 Lift the bundles of asparagus out of the pan, drain them thoroughly, and untie them. Serve the asparagus piping hot on a white napkin. Set out the jug of vinaigrette, a dish of rough salt, a pepper mill and bread for mopping. That's all.

SERVING SUGGESTIONS FOR ASPARAGUS ~ If you would rather serve the asparagus cold, accompany it with mayonnaise (see page 163). France's northerners – those who live in dairy country – prefer their asparagus served hot and sauced with melted butter or hollandaise sauce (see page 248).

cèpes à la bordelaise

SAUTÉED CEPS

B oletus edulis, *most prized of the many varieties of edible wild fungi gathered throughout the woods and forests of Europe, are known in France as cèpes or bolets, in Italy as porcini, in Britain as penny buns or boletus. Large, meaty, firm-fleshed fungi, the edible members of the family are distinguished by their brown caps and spongy yellow underparts. A single cep can weigh half a kilo, though they weigh heavier if gathered on a wet day. They are gathered in the woods and forests of the northern hemisphere from mid-July until the first frosts of winter. The inhabitants of Bordeaux value them particularly highly and cook them in olive oil with garlic or shallots and parsley.*

Serves 4

about 500g (1lb 2oz) ceps (at least 1 large cep per person)
4–5 tablespoons olive oil
salt and freshly milled pepper
4 tablespoons chopped flat-leaf parsley
2 garlic cloves or shallots, finely chopped
about 2 tablespoons fresh breadcrumbs

1 Ceps are magnets for creepy-crawlies, so inspect the fungi and remove any unwelcome interlopers. Trim the stalks sparingly, scraping off any moss and earth. Wipe the caps but do not rinse them unless they really need it. If your specimens are overly mature and dark, or were picked on a damp day, remove the spongy underparts. Slice.

2 Heat the oil in a roomy frying pan. When the oil is hot but not smoking, put in the prepared ceps and sprinkle with a little salt to start the juices running. Fry for 5 minutes or so, until the edges of the slices begin to sizzle and brown – the time this takes depends on how wet the fungi were to begin with.

3 Add the garlic and parsley, and allow all to cook together gently for another 5 minutes. Stir in enough breadcrumbs to absorb all the juices. Turn the heat up for a moment to gild the breadcrumbs. That's all.

champignons à la grecque

MARINATED MUSHROOMS

A little salad of button mushrooms dressed with lemon juice and olive oil – this is modest but good. The cultivated mushroom, a descendent of Agaricus campestris, the common field mushroom, is known in France as champignon de Paris since it was commercially produced on the disused racecourses of Paris, abandoned in the aftermath of the Revolution.

Serves 4

350g (12oz) very fresh button mushrooms
150ml (¼ pint) white wine
2 tablespoons olive oil
1 tablespoon lemon juice
1 teaspoon coriander seeds
pinch of dried thyme
1–2 bay leaves, crumbled

TO FINISH
1 tablespoon chopped parsley

1 Wipe the mushrooms, slice finely and then spread them in a shallow dish.

2 Bring the remaining ingredients to the boil in a small pan and bubble up for 1–2 minutes, until the steam no longer smells of raw alcohol. Tip the contents of the pan over the mushrooms and leave to marinate overnight. Finish with parsley.

NOTE ~ To vary the flavour and add colour, finish with 2–3 tablespoons chopped, peeled and seeded tomato.

croustade aux chanterelles

CHANTERELLE TART

A recipe from Provence, for which the tart base is made with an olive-oil pastry. Any wild or cultivated fungi can be substituted for the chanterelles, a late summer crop found under beech trees and in and around birch woods: look for their bright orange frills tucked under the leaf mould. Later in the autumn, choose a mixture of pied de mouton, hedgehog fungi, cèpes, boletus and trompette de la mort, horn of plenty.

Serves 4 as a starter

250g (9oz) plain flour
4 tablespoons olive oil
½ teaspoon salt

FILLING
2 tablespoons olive oil
350g (12oz) chanterelles or button mushrooms, sliced
1 large onion, finely sliced
1 thyme sprig
2 tablespoons chopped black olives
4 eggs
100g (4oz) fresh goat's cheese
salt and freshly milled pepper

1 Work the flour, olive oil and salt for the pastry together vigorously with the hook of your hand, adding enough warm water to form a smooth ball which comes away from the sides of the mixing bowl. Flatten the ball of dough a little, cover with cling film and set it to rest for 30 minutes, while you prepare the filling.

2 For the filling, heat the oil gently in a frying pan, add the chanterelles, onion and thyme and fry gently until the fungi yield their juice and begins to sizzle. When they all begin to brown a little, stir in the olives. Remove from the heat, pick out the thyme and leave to cool.

3 Preheat the oven to 200°C (400°F, gas 6). Roll out the pastry to fit a 25cm (10in) round tart tin. Prick the base and bake for 10–15 minutes, until the pastry is set. If the pastry bubbles, prick it again.

4 Meanwhile, beat the eggs with the soft cheese, plenty of black pepper and a little salt. Stir in the fungi mixture. Spread this filling in the tart case. Reduce the oven temperature to 180°C (350°F, gas 4) and bake the tart for 35–40 minutes, until the filling is almost set but still a little trembly in the middle.

morilles à la crème

MOREL MUSHROOMS *with* CREAM

The morel, *Morcella esculenta*, is a spring mushroom, a lover not of woodland but of open spaces, found in rough pasture and on roadside verges. I have often found it in association with ground orchids, a species which likes the same habitat. The morel has a distinctive wrinkled cap and a fragrance almost as seductive as the truffle. It dries well without losing texture and flavour and in a sauce or stew dried is actually superior to fresh – 25g (1oz) dried is equivalent to 150g (5oz) fresh.

Serves 4

350g (12oz) fresh morels
50g (2oz) unsalted butter
salt
1 tablespoon chopped parsley
pinch of dried thyme
150ml (¼ pint) crème fraîche
freshly milled pepper
4 thick slices pain de campagne or robust
country bread, such as sour-dough bread

1 Shake out any grit from the morels, slice off the woody ends of the stalks and slice the little honeycombed caps.

2 Heat a little knob of butter in a small pan, add the fungi and fry for 2–3 minutes, until their juices begin to run. Sprinkle with a little salt, the parsley and a pinch of thyme, and fry until the fungi sizzle and brown a little. Stir in the crème fraîche, season with pepper and bubble up for another couple of minutes.

3 Meanwhile, toast 4 slices of the bread. Pile the cream-sauced morels on the toast and finish with another turn of the pepper mill.

NOTE ~ Failing fresh morels (available at good delis or specialist greengrocers), substitute a few dried morels, pre-soaked in a little water and combined with oyster mushrooms.

topinambours à la provençale

JERUSALEM ARTICHOKES *with* GARLIC AND OLIVES

The Jerusalem or root artichoke is a New World member of the daisy family, a group that includes the merry sunflower. The Italian for sunflower is girasole, hence 'Jerusalem'. The sweetness in the flesh is inulin, a natural sugar which can be eaten by diabetics. Their knobbly shape make Jerusalem artichokes tricky to peel: boil them in salted water for 10 minutes, then rub off the papery skin.

Serves 4

500g (1lb 2oz) Jerusalem artichokes, peeled or not, as preferred
2 tablespoons olive oil
1 tablespoon black olives, pitted or not, as preferred
2 tablespoons lemon juice
1 teaspoon finely grated lemon zest
75ml (3fl oz) white wine
about 150ml (¼ pint) chicken or vegetable stock
¼ teaspoon freshly grated nutmeg
freshly milled pepper
1 garlic clove, chopped
2 tablespoons chopped parsley

1 Cut the artichokes into walnut-sized pieces, rinse and transfer to a casserole or saucepan. Add the olive oil, olives, lemon juice and zest and wine and enough stock to barely cover the pieces. Season with nutmeg and pepper – no salt yet.

2 Bring to the boil, turn down the heat, cover and cook the artichokes until tender – 25–30 minutes. Take the lid off and let any liquid boil away, so that the artichokes fry a little.

3 Stir in the garlic and parsley and bubble-fry for another minute. Taste and add salt if needed – unlikely, as the olives are quite salty enough. Serve at room temperature.

artichauts à la barigoule

ARTICHOKES COOKED LIKE TRUFFLES

Throughout the summer in Provençal markets, artichokes are sold on their stalks in great bunches for little more than the price of a cabbage, allowing cooks to be as profligate as they please. Better still, for a little extra, the hearts can be bought ready prepared. The aromatic cooking broth in this recipe is designed to give the artichokes the flavour of the barigoule, *a pale-fleshed summer truffle.*

Serves 4–6

8–12 artichoke hearts plus the upper stalks
4 tablespoons olive oil
1 large onion, finely chopped
2–3 garlic cloves, finely chopped
1 carrot, finely chopped
1–2 celery sticks, finely chopped
3 tablespoons finely chopped black olives
2 tablespoons chopped jambon cru (raw cured ham)
or lean bacon
1 glass white wine
salt and freshly milled pepper
a little sugar
1–2 dried or fresh thyme sprigs, crumbled or chopped
2 dried or fresh sage leaves, crumbled or chopped
1–2 bay leaves

TO FINISH
1 tablespoon chopped parsley
2–3 tablespoons fresh breadcrumbs

1 Quarter the prepared artichoke hearts (see page 64). Trim and scrape the stalks to remove the inedible stringy outer layer and chop the tender centre into short bean-sized lengths.

2 Heat the olive oil in a heavy pan or flameproof casserole. Add the onion and garlic and fry gently until they take a little colour. Add the carrot, celery, olives, ham or bacon and herbs and fry for a few minutes more.

3 Pour in the wine and a glass of water and bubble up. Stir in the artichoke pieces – hearts and stalks – and bubble up again. Turn down the heat, season with salt, pepper and a little sugar, and cover loosely. Leave to simmer for 30–40 minutes until the artichokes are perfectly tender. Alternatively, preheat the oven to 180°C (350°F, gas 4), cover the casserole (with foil if necessary) and cook in the oven for 45 minutes.

4 Check during cooking in case the vegetables need a little more water. By the end, the liquid should have reduced to an aromatic few tablespoons. If there is too much liquid, bubble it up fiercely to evaporate the excess. Stir in the parsley and enough fresh breadcrumbs to take up all the juice. Serve at room temperature.

TO PREPARE AN ARTICHOKE HEART ~ Have ready a bowl of cold water and squeeze in the juice of ½ lemon. Rinse the artichoke and trim off the stalk close to the base. Scrape the stalk to remove the hard exterior fibres (the tender centre can be eaten) and drop it into the lemon water so it does not discolour.

Snap off the tough outer leaves, then, with a sharp knife, cut off the tops of the remaining leaves within 1cm/½in of the base. Nick out the inner leaves, exposing the hairy choke. Remove the choke, scraping it out with a sharp spoon, and drop the prepared base into the water. The artichoke heart is now ready for cooking.

The artichoke, a member of the thistle family native to the shores of the Mediterranean, produces a chemical, cynarin, which has the effect of making anything which is drunk afterwards taste sweeter – a disadvantage for wine-drinkers but pleasant for those who drink water. So noticeable is this effect that the plant acquired a bad reputation in Caesar's Rome, where the naturalist Pliny complained of its evil effects. The plant is also one of several capable of turning milk into curds for cheese-making, providing a replacement for animal rennet, a digestive organism found in the stomachs of all lactating mammals, including – lest we give ourselves airs above our station – ourselves. Take advantage of the association by serving plain-boiled artichokes with a little sauce of fresh cream cheese, well-seasoned and flavoured with herbs, to spoon into the choke when you've eaten the tender bases of the leaves dipped in a vinaigrette. Allow 20–30 minutes in boiling salted water, depending on the size of artichokes, and when you're ready to eat the heart, don't forget to lift out the hairy little choke with a sharp knife. To prepare the cream cheese, beat 250g (8oz) fresh curd cheese with half its own volume of crème fraîche, season with salt and freshly milled black pepper, and beat in a finely chopped garlic clove and a tablespoon each of chopped parsley, chives and chervil.

soufflé au fromage

CHEESE SOUFFLÉ

This is the classic French soufflé, the simplest and the easiest since the cheese blends smoothly with the egg and does not inhibit the rise. The shape and volume of the cooking dish matters. For this recipe you need a soufflé mould (a straight-sided, round ovenproof china or Pyrex dish), diameter 20–22cm (8–9in). Size is important, as are the straight sides that allow the soufflé to rise evenly above the edge.

Serves 4

50g (2oz) butter
50g (2oz) plain flour
275ml (9fl oz) milk
100g (4oz) mature cheese, such as Cantal or Gruyère, grated
¼ teaspoon freshly grated nutmeg
salt and freshly milled pepper
1 tablespoon grated Parmesan cheese
5 eggs, separated

1 First make a béchamel sauce, the basis for all savoury soufflés. Over a low heat, melt the butter in a small heavy-based saucepan, sprinkle in the flour and cook gently for 2–3 minutes until the mixture looks sandy. Whisk in the milk using a wire whisk or beat with a wooden spoon until the sauce is smooth and thick.

2 Beat in the mature cheese. Season with the nutmeg, salt and pepper and leave to cool.

3 Meanwhile, prepare a double-thick collar of greaseproof paper about the width of your hand, and tie it firmly around the outside of the 20–22cm (8–9in) diameter souffle mould with string. Butter the inside of both the dish and the collar, and dust with the Parmesan.

4 Preheat the oven to 400°F (200°C, gas 6). As soon as the béchamel has cooled, beat in the egg yolks. Whisk the egg whites until stiff but do not over-whisk them or they will become dry and grainy. Fold the whites lightly into the béchamel mixture with a metal spoon. Do not be scared to mix thoroughly, just use light strokes and lift the spoon to make sure you incorporate air.

5 Tip the mixture into the soufflé mould and run a knife around the edge just inside the rim to encourage rising. Bake for 30 minutes without opening the oven door. Remove from the oven as soon as the soufflé is beautifully puffed. Snip the string to release the paper collar and serve without delay.

VARIATIONS ~ Other flavourings that can replace or augment the cheese are finely chopped spinach or ham, flaked crab, chopped shrimp or mushrooms sautéed in butter.

croque monsieur

TOASTED CHEESE AND HAM SANDWICH

France's favourite toastie was first served, says Larousse Gastronomique, in 1910 in a café in Paris, the Boulevard de Capucines, and remains a popular café snack throughout the land. As a hot hors d'œuvre, it has the advantage of being quickly prepared with ingredients easily to hand. The desirable crunchiness that gives the preparation its name is best achieved by frying in butter with a little olive oil. You may, if you wish, butter the bread on both sides and toast it instead. The ham can be replaced by cooked chicken. When topped with a poached egg, monsieur becomes madame – for reasons I'm sure you can work out for yourself.

Serves 4

8 slices day-old bread off a sandwich loaf or tin loaf
about 100g (4oz) unsalted butter, softened
4 slices mature cheese, such as Cantal or Gruyère
4 slices smoked ham
2–3 tablespoons olive oil

1 Spread the bread lightly with softened butter – you'll need about half – and sandwich them together with the cheese and ham. Remove the crusts.

2 Melt the remaining butter with the olive oil in a frying pan. Fry the sandwiches over a medium heat, turning them once, until the cheese has melted and the bread is deliciously crisp and brown.

NOTE ~ For a more substantial dish – a light lunch or simple supper – cover the finished croques with a cheese-flavoured bechamel, sprinkle with grated cheese and slip under a preheated grill to bubble and brown.

salade de fromage de chèvre chaud

WARM GOAT'S CHEESE SALAD

This simple little salad is the standby of every rural restaurant in the southern regions of France – goat-country – where the little curd-cheeses known as tommes (a name also applied to similar preparations of sheep's and cow's milk) are traditionally prepared and sold by the goat-keepers themselves. Creamy little cakes about the size of a baby's fist of freshly pressed curd, you will see them displayed on trays in every marketplace. They are sold plain, or dusted with thyme, rosemary or crushed multi-coloured peppercorns. They are also sold at various stages of maturity – bloomed, wrinkled or hardened. The fresh tommes needed for this recipe have not had a chance to mature and they taste of the particular herbs and leaves that have pastured the goats. The flavour is so place-specific that a local palate would expect to be able to distinguish between a fresh tomme made from the milk of a flock pastured on one or other side of the mountain.

Serves 4

2 well-drained tommes or small fresh goat's cheese
4 slices day-old baguette
about 6 tablespoons olive oil
1 frissee lettuce (curly endive) or any bitter salad leaves
1 large cube stale bread, rubbed with garlic
about 2 tablespoons wine vinegar
1 teaspoon sea salt (sel de Guerande, for the flavour)

1 Preheat the grill or the oven to 220°C (425°F, gas 7). Split the cheeses in half horizontally. Toast the baguette slices lightly on both sides, trickle with oil and top each with a round of cheese.

2 Place the salad leaves in a salad bowl with the garlic-rubbed bread. (This is the chapon: an integral part of the French salad bowl, it is designed to perfume the leaves but is never eaten.)

3 Mix the vinegar with the salt and work it with a fork until the granules dissolve. Then fork in the olive oil. Toss the salad with this dressing.

4 Place the cheese-topped bread rounds in the hot oven for 3–4 minutes to melt and bubble, or toast them under the grill. Slip them on to the salad and serve without delay (take care not to eat the chapon).

soups

consommé

CLEAR BEEF BROTH

A basic beef broth which has been concentrated, fortified and clarified, this is one of those simple preparations by which you can judge the excellence of a chef's kitchen. A consommé can be served plain, or used as the basis for other soups, veloutés and broths.

Makes about 1.5 litres (4 pints)

2kg (4½lb) beef bones, chopped into chunks
1 chicken carcass (bones only) or 500g (1lb 2oz) chicken wings
500g (1lb 2oz) carrots, scraped and chunked
500g (1lb 2oz) leeks, rinsed and chunked
2 onions, unpeeled but quartered
2–3 celery sticks, cut into chunks
a small bunch of bay, parsley and thyme
½ teaspoon white peppercorns
salt

TO FORTIFY
1kg (2¼lb) lean shin of beef, cut into chunks
1 tablespoon chopped tomato (optional)

TO CLARIFY
3 egg whites, well whisked

1 Preheat the oven to 180°C (350°F, gas 4). Place the beef bones in a roomy roasting tin and bake for 30 minutes, until well browned.

2 Transfer the bones to a large soup pot. Add the chicken carcass, carrots, leeks, onions, celery, herbs and peppercorns. Pour in 3 litres (5 pints) water. Bring gently to the boil, allow one big belch and turn down the heat so that the liquid simmers. Cover loosely and leave to cook gently for 2 hours or so, until well flavoured and strong. The surface of the liquid should tremble, no more.

3 Strain the broth, discard the solids and leave the broth to cool, overnight if possible. Skim off the fat that rises and solidifies overnight.

4 To fortify the broth, return it to the pot and add the shin of beef. Bring to the boil and leave to cook gently for another 2 hours, until the meat has given up all its goodness and the broth has reduced by half. If the colour is not sufficiently golden, add the chopped tomato.

5 Strain, discarding the bones and return the broth to the pot. (Save the meat for a Hashis Parmentier, see page 214.) Whisk in the egg whites, bring back to the boil and simmer for 20 minutes. The egg white will float to the surface, collecting all the impurities on the way and leaving a broth of sparkling clarity.

6 Remove from the heat and strain through a fine muslin cloth. Blot the surface of the broth with kitchen paper laid over the surface to pick up any golden bubbles of fat that have survived the clarifying. Serve the consommé elegantly, in double-handled soup cups.

CONSOMMÉ OF GOOD COLOUR ~ The preliminary caramelisation of the sugars naturally present in the bone meat during the short roasting, along with the natural colour of the onion skins and carrots, will give the broth an appetising golden tint.

JELLIED CONSOMMÉ ~ In summer, leave the soup to cool, chill overnight and serve as a jellied consommé – very Marcel Proust.

The importance of understanding how to prepare a good consommé cannot be exaggerated – or so chefs of the old school will tell you. Forget the stock cubes, leave the little cartons of ready-made where they belong – on the supermarket shelf. I had my first lesson in the etiquette of the stock-pot in the 1980s, at a time when French was still the language of the kitchen and a training in haute cuisine was the sum of a young chef's ambition – before Fusion took over where Italianate left off. At the time, new to the world of recipe-writing and curious to understand the difference between the domestic and the professional kitchen, I spent a working day in the subterranean kitchen of Michel Bourdin, chef de cuisine at the Connaught Hotel in London. In those days, they didn't come much more professional than Chef Bourdin. The day started at dawn – around 6.30 am in early September – with the preparation of the bones for the stock which would serve as the basis for the consommé to be served that evening in the restaurant. Enormous trays of gigantic red-hot bones were whirled around the kitchen with scrupulous politeness by brawny-armed chefs whose qualifications seemed better suited to weight-lifting than dainty behaviour with a whisk. The spitting, steaming mass, smelling deliciously of caramelised meat, was tipped into vats the size of a sherry-barrel and left to bubble and brood all day. These preliminaries were, however, as nothing compared to the Herculean labour of straining and clarifying, a task which involved the entire brawny-armed brigade. "And that," said Michel Bourdin, sipping his tasting-spoon with satisfaction, "is the difference between the housewife and the chef."

velouté de volaille

CREAM OF CHICKEN SOUP

This velvet-smooth chicken soup thickened with egg yolk and enriched with cream is one of the glories of the French kitchen. A strong, home-made chicken broth is the secret.

Serves 4

900ml (1½ pints) chicken broth
1 boneless chicken breast, skinned
3 egg yolks
about 6 tablespoons crème fraîche
25g (1oz) unsalted butter
25g (1oz) plain flour
¼ teaspoon freshly grated nutmeg
salt and freshly milled pepper

1 Heat the chicken broth until it is boiling. Add the chicken breast and poach it for 8–12 minutes, depending on size, until firm and cooked right through.

2 Remove the chicken breast and shred it roughly. Reserve a tablespoonful of the shreds, puree the remainder in a blender with a ladleful of the broth, the egg yolks and the cream until smooth and liquid. Reserve this puree.

3 Melt the butter in a roomy saucepan, stir in the flour and fry until the mixture is sandy, but do not let it brown. Gradually whisk in the broth and simmer gently until it thickens.

4 Remove the pan from the heat and whisk in the pureed chicken and cream mixture. Reheat gently, whisking all the while, until the soup is just below boiling point. Taste and season with nutmeg, salt and pepper. Return the reserved shredded chicken to the soup and serve without reheating.

VARIATION ~ To make a velouté with asparagus or artichoke hearts, prepare the vegetables as usual, removing all woody bits, and poach them in the broth instead of the chicken breast. Finish as in the main recipe, pureeing the vegetables with the cream and egg yolks.

potage germiny

CHILLED SORREL SOUP

Gather your own sorrel from the wild if you can't find it anywhere else – the pointed, heart-shaped dark green leaves are unmistakeable. Although the substitution of watercress and a squeeze of lemon juice will fool all but the keenest palate, once you've acquired a taste for its refreshing sharpness, nothing else will do.

Serves 4–6

2 generous handfuls sorrel leaves, rinsed and shredded
25g (1oz) butter
900ml (1½ pints) strong chicken stock
25g (1oz) plain flour
150ml (¼ pint) crème fraîche
salt and freshly milled pepper

TO FINISH
a little crème fraîche
a few sorrel leaves, shredded
croutons, fried in olive oil and butter

1 Place the sorrel in a pan with a pinch of salt and the butter. Cover tightly and shake over the heat for 2–3 minutes, until the leaves collapse.

2 Puree the contents of the pan in a blender with the chicken stock and flour until smooth. (Alternatively, finely chop the sorrel, mix it with the flour and add the stock.) Pour the mixture back into the pan and bring to the boil, whisking until the soup thickens a little and no longer tastes of raw flour.

3 Whisk in the crème fraîche. Check the seasoning and add salt and pepper. Remove the pan from the heat and leave to cool. Then chill the soup.

4 Serve the chilled soup topped with a swirl of cream and a curl of shredded fresh sorrel. For a contrast of texture, hand a bowl of hot croutons separately.

soupe à l'oignon

ONION SOUP

A clear bone broth, thick with onions, was the early-morning refreshment in Les Halles, Paris's meat-market. The market has now moved to the outskirts, but when it was at Les Halles in the city centre (and still there in the late 1950s) students from the Sorbonne (myself on occasion among them) would join the porters and wholesalers at the communal wooden tables in the surrounding cafés. A marmite – a deep, round-bellied earthenware cooking pot – is the traditional implement for a heavy, slow simmered soup such as this.

Serves 4–6

750g (1lb 10oz) onions, very finely sliced in rings
75g (3oz) butter
150ml (¼ pint) white wine
600ml (1 pint) strong beef-bone stock
salt and freshly milled pepper

TO FINISH
about 175g (6oz) cheese, such as Cantal, Gruyère or Emmenthal
4–6 thick slices day-old baguette

1 Fry the onions in the butter. Cook them very gently, stirring every now and then, for at least 20 minutes, until they are soft and golden.

2 Add the wine. Bring to the boil and bubble up for a few minutes to evaporate the alcohol. Pour in the stock and 300ml (½ pint) cold water, and season with salt and pepper. Bring back to the boil and turn the heat down to simmer the soup. Leave on a low heat for 20 minutes.

3 Meanwhile, preheat the oven to 150°C (300°F, gas 2). Put the baguette slices in the oven to dry. Divide the bread among soup bowls, then ladle in the hot soup: the bread will rise to the top. Either preheat the grill and grate the cheese on to the bread, then place the bowls under the grill to melt and brown the cheese, or hand out the cheese and grater for people to add their own, as they liked it in Les Halles.

NOTE ~ For a more substantial soup, thicken the cooked broth with 2 eggs beaten with a ladleful of the hot soup, and reheat without boiling.

vichyssoise

CHILLED LEEK AND POTATO SOUP

A recipe of relatively modern date (a century, no more), this is a refinement of the classic leek and potato soup invented by a French chef from the Bourbonnais working in the US. In the original, the enrichment is butter rather than cream, and it is served hot rather than chilled. Vichyssoise is good with radishes and hot, buttery garlic bread.

Serves 4–6

2 large leeks, white part only, finely sliced
2 large potatoes, peeled and cut into chunks
a small bunch of bay, thyme and parsley
150ml (¼ pint) crème fraîche
salt and freshly milled pepper

TO FINISH
snipped chives

1 Simmer the leeks and potatoes in 1 litre (¾ pint) water with the herbs and a little salt for 30–40 minutes, until very tender.

2 Remove the herbs and puree the soup until smooth in a blender. Taste and add salt and pepper. Cool, then whisk in the crème fraîche and chill the soup. Finish with a sprinkling of chives when serving.

GARLIC BREAD ~ To prepare garlic bread, cut diagonal slits in a day-old baguette and fill the slashes with unsalted butter mashed with a little garlic – the fresher the garlic, the gentler the flavour. Wrap the baguette in foil or not, as you please: unwrapped, the crust will be crispier; the risk is the loss of some of the butter. Pop the baguette in an oven preheated to 180°C (350°F, gas 4) and heat for about 20 minutes, until the butter has melted and soaked into the crumb.

vegetables

pommes de terre sautées

SAUTÉED POTATOES

P otatoes, butter and parsley are all you need for this
sumptuous little recipe from northern France, dairy-
country, where butter – rather than the olive oil of the south
or the goose fat of central France – is the frying fat of choice.
French unsalted butter produces very little residue when melted,
giving it a relatively high burn point, which makes it perfect
for a high-heat sauté – a term which, translated literally,
means jump-in-the-pan. Sautéed potatoes are good with
grilled lamb cutlets or a steak finished with maître-d'hôtel
butter (see page 252).

∾

Serves 4

1kg (2¼lb) potatoes, scrubbed not peeled
100g (4oz) unsalted butter
salt and freshly milled pepper
2 tablespoons chopped flat-leaf parsley

1 Cook the potatoes until soft in enough boiling salted water to cover them generously. This takes 20 minutes or so. Drain the potatoes, return them to the pan and shake over the heat to dry them out completely. Set the potatoes aside off the heat. Peel them as soon as they are cool enough to handle and slice thickly.

2 Melt the butter in a roomy sauté pan or heavy frying pan. Put in the potato slices, season with salt and pepper, and fry briskly for 8–10 minutes, turning the slices carefully to brown both sides. Sprinkle with parsley just before serving.

pommes de terre à la boulangère

BREAD-OVEN POTATOES

I n the old days, before ordinary households acquired their own ovens, dishes such as this one that required baking — a luxurious method — were taken to the village baker's cooling oven after the day's bread-baking was done. The service was offered for a small fee and the title persists though the service is no longer required.

Serves 4–6

50g (2oz) butter
2 onions, finely sliced
100g (4oz) streaky bacon, diced
1kg (2¼lb) potatoes, peeled and thinly sliced
½ teaspoon thyme leaves
1 small piece bay leaf, crumbled
about 600ml (1 pint) boiling stock (chicken, beef or vegetable)

1 Preheat the oven to 180°C (350°F, gas 4). Heat the butter in a frying pan and fry the onions and bacon until the onions are lightly browned.

2 Layer the potatoes, bacon and onion mixture and herbs in a roomy gratin dish. Pour in enough boiling stock to cover the ingredients completely.

3 Cover the dish with foil, shiny side down. Transfer to the oven and bake for 30 minutes. Remove the foil and bake for a further 15–30 minutes, until the potatoes are tender and browned on top.

gratin dauphinois

POTATOES BAKED *with* CREAM

This is one of the most delicious and simplest of all potato dishes. The combination of cream and potatoes needs nothing more than a light seasoning with garlic and nutmeg. No cheese, no eggs, though traditionalists usually include a finely sliced turnip. The thickness of the potato slices dictates the time it takes to cook.

∽

Serves 4–6

1kg (2¼lb) waxy potatoes, peeled and sliced
1 garlic clove
1 small turnip, peeled and finely sliced
salt and freshly milled pepper
½ teaspoon freshly grated nutmeg
about 600ml (1 pint) single cream
a walnut-sized nugget of butter

1 Preheat the oven to 150°C (300°F, gas 2). Choose a gratin dish just large and deep enough to accommodate the potato slices in 3–4 layers. Cut the garlic in two and rub it around the dish. Lay the potato and turnip slices in the dish, sprinkling between the layers with salt, pepper and nutmeg.

2 Heat the cream until boiling and pour it over the potatoes, adding just enough to submerge the slices. Dot with a few scraps of butter and cover tightly with a lid or foil, shiny side down.

3 Bake for 1–1½ hours, until the potatoes are perfectly tender and have drunk up almost all the cream. Test for tenderness with a knife after 1 hour. For the final 15 minutes, uncover and turn up the heat to 200–220°C (400–425°F, gas 6–7) so the top browns and bubbles.

pommes de terre mousseline

CREAMY MASHED POTATOES

France's mashed potatoes are enriched with egg yolk and cream, and flavoured with nutmeg – they are far richer and more delicious than English mash. Choose medium potatoes of the same size so they cook evenly. If the potatoes are very large, do not boil them but bake them in their jackets and scoop out the soft interior.

Serves 4–6

1kg (2¼lb) potatoes, scrubbed not peeled
175g (6oz) unsalted butter, softened
4 egg yolks
200ml (7fl oz) whipping cream, whipped
salt and freshly milled white pepper
½ teaspoon freshly grated nutmeg

TO FINISH (OPTIONAL)
chopped fresh herbs, such as parsley, chervil and/or chives
a little melted butter

1 Cook the potatoes in plenty of boiling salted water until perfectly tender – 25–30 minutes. Drain thoroughly and shake them over the heat for a moment to evaporate excess moisture.

2 As soon as they are cool enough to handle, peel the potatoes and push them through a mouli-legumes, potato ricer, or mash and sieve them. Return the mash to the pan, reheat gently and beat in the butter. Remove from the heat and beat in the egg yolks. Fold in the whipped cream. Taste and season with salt, pepper and nutmeg.

3 To serve plain, pile in a warm dish and finish with a shower of chopped green herbs. To serve with a crisp topping, first preheat the oven to 200°C (400°F, gas 6). Spread the potatoes in a gratin dish, sprinkle with melted butter and bake for 10 minutes, until lightly browned and bubbling.

DUCHESSE POTATOES ~ Omit the finishing cream and use a star-shaped piping nozzle to pipe little pyramids of the hot mousseline on to a buttered baking sheet, sprinkle with a little melted butter and bake as above.

POTATO CROQUETTES ~ Allow the mousseline to cool and firm before forming it into little cork-shaped patties. Roll the patties lightly in flour, dip them in egg and breadcrumbs, and set aside for 10 minutes to allow the coating to firm. Then deep fry until brown and crisp.

pommes de terre salardaises

POTATOES BROWNED IN GOOSE DRIPPING

P otatoes browned in confit fat, this is a winter recipe from the Périgord, the land of the fattened goose. When served with a grilled magret de canard or d'oie (duck or goose breast), it is the defining dish of the region. You can buy goose fat in a tin (a cheaper option than buying the whole confit) or save the drippings when roasting your Christmas goose or Sunday duck. If you roast the bird on a rack set over a roasting tin with a little water, the fat will stay white and won't burn. As a special treat during the black truffle season (late November to early March) you might like to include a few slivers of fresh truffle.

Serves 4

3 tablespoons goose or duck dripping
1kg (2¼lb) potatoes, peeled and cut into bite-sized chunks
4 garlic cloves, cut into slivers, or 1 large onion, sliced into
fine half-moons
salt and freshly milled pepper
2 tablespoons chopped flat-leaf parsley

1 Heat the dripping in a roomy sauté pan. As soon as the fat begins to sizzle and yield up its water, add the potatoes and toss over a gentle heat for 10 minutes, until they begin to brown.

2 Add the garlic or onion and a wine glass of water. Season with salt and pepper, bubble up and cook gently for another 10–15 minutes. Break up the potatoes with a fork, crumbling them a little as soon as they soften, but do not mash.

3 Continue to cook gently, stirring, until the water has evaporated and everything starts to fry again. Stir in the parsley and remove from the heat. The potatoes should have absorbed all the goose fat, retained a little shape, and be deliciously golden and soft.

aligot

POTATOES *with* CHEESE

A remarkable dish from the ravines of the Auvergne, this is traditionally served at weddings. Peasant cooking at its most robust: when this dish appears on elegant restaurant menus (as it sometimes does), you can be sure the chef is from the region and had the recipe from his granny. The correct cheese is the local tomme de Cantal, though Emmenthal or Gruyère will do. The more you beat it, the lighter it will be.

Serves 4–6

1kg (2¼lb) floury potatoes
1 garlic clove, halved
150ml (¼ pint) double cream
100g (4oz) unsalted butter, diced
500g (1lb 2oz) tomme de Cantal, cut into slivers
salt

1 Boil the potatoes in their jackets in enough salted water to cover. Start with cold water and, about 20 minutes after the water reaches the boil, when perfectly tender, drain the potatoes. Leave until just cool enough to handle.

2 Slip off their skins and return the potatoes to the pan. Set the pan over a low heat and mash the potatoes thoroughly.

3 Meanwhile, rub a heavy pan with the cut side of the garlic clove (discard the rest – a little garlic goes a long way and you don't want to drown the flavour of the cheese). In the garlicky pan, bring the cream and the butter gently to the boil. As soon as the butter melts, beat in the mashed potato.

4 When the potatoes are steaming, add the cheese and beat it in with a wooden spoon or spatula, lifting the utensil high to incorporate as much air as possible. Serve as soon as the cheese has completely melted and the mixture is light and fluffy, as it rapidly loses its volume.

SERVING TIP ~ Aligot is delicious but rich. If you value your digestion, don't serve it with wine or anything chilled. Instead, advise your guests to take nothing until they have eaten their fill. Then pour them a nip of white brandy – eau de vie de prune, framboise or poire – to settle the stomach.

petits pois à la française

BABY PEAS *with* ONIONS AND LETTUCE

A dish of slow-simmered peas, this is always served as a separate course, handed around after the meat. The long, gentle cooking works its magic on frozen peas as well as fresh.

Serves 4

750g (1lb 10oz) shelled young peas
12 very small baby onions, skinned
1 small romaine or cos lettuce, shredded
a few parsley and chervil sprigs, tied in a bunch
150ml (¼ pint) white wine or water (or a mixture)
a walnut-sized nugget of unsalted butter
1 tablespoon sugar
1 teaspoon salt

TO FINISH
a walnut-sized nugget of unsalted butter,
chopped in small pieces

1 Put all the ingredients (except the butter for finishing) in a heavy-based pan. Bring to the boil and bubble up for a moment to evaporate the alcohol if using wine.

2 Cover and simmer gently for 30–40 minutes, until the peas have lost their fresh green colour and the cooking juices are reduced to a couple of tablespoonfuls. Remove the bunch of herbs and stir in the finishing butter.

VARIATIONS ~ For petits pois à la bonne femme, proceed as above, but omit the lettuce. Replace the wine with chicken stock and include a tablespoon of diced raw ham or lean bacon.

For petits pois à la fermiére, proceed as above, but include a handful of baby carrots.

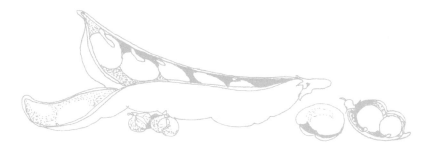

confit d'oignons

CARAMELISED ONIONS

Mild, sweet red onions are becoming widely available – although you can make this with ordinary onions if you cannot find reds. Make this a day ahead if you like but no sooner.

Makes about 600ml (1 pint)

2oz (50g) unsalted butter
6 tablespoons brown sugar
6 large red onions, finely sliced
2 tablespoons red wine vinegar
2 tablespoons red wine
1 tablespoon honey
salt and freshly milled white pepper

1 Melt the butter in a heavy pan and stir in the sugar. Stir over a medium heat for 10 minutes (as if making fudge – if that helps to explain). When the mixture caramelises to a light brown, stir in the sliced onions, vinegar and wine. Add a splash of water and bring to the boil.

2 Turn down the heat, cover and leave to simmer for another 15 minutes, until the onions are soft. Remove from the heat, season, and stir in the honey.

puree d'ail à la crème

GARLIC PUREE *with* CREAM

Fragrant, smooth, rich and delicate, this puree is the perfect accompaniment for plain-grilled meats or spooned over a fried egg. Best made with fresh garlic, whose cloves have just formed, when the covering will still be soft and the cloves plump and mild-flavoured. If using elderly garlic, halve the cloves first and nick out the little green sprout at the heart.

Serves 4–6

10 heads fresh garlic
150ml (¼ pint) double cream
salt and freshly milled pepper

1 Peel the garlic cloves and put them in enough boiling salted water to cover. Let them simmer for 10 minutes. Drain. If the garlic is a little elderly, allow another 5 minutes.

2 Puree the garlic by pushing it through a mouli-légume, potato ricer, and then beat in the cream. Alternatively, puree both garlic and cream in a blender until smooth. Reheat to serve and season with salt and pepper.

tomates à la provençale

TOMATOES SLOW-COOKED *with* GARLIC

A simple recipe, but perfect of its kind. The tomatoes can only achieve their concentrated sweetness through long slow cooking – allow them all the time they need. This is delicious served with braised fennel (see opposite).

Serves 4

8 large ripe beef tomatoes
3 tablespoons olive oil
2 garlic cloves, peeled
salt
a handful of flat-leaf parsley

1 Cut the tomatoes in half and remove the seeds. Warm the
oil in a wide shallow pan. Put the tomatoes in the pan, cut
sides down. Fry the tomatoes over the gentlest of heat for
40–45 minutes, shaking the pan from time to time so that they
do not stick and burn.

2 Crush the garlic with salt, and then mince it very finely with
the parsley. Turn the tomatoes over, and sprinkle them with
salt, garlic and parsley. Let them continue to cook very, very
gently on the other side – another 30 minutes is not too long.

BRAISED FENNEL ~ To braise fennel: trim and quarter the
bulbs and lay them in a single layer in a gratin dish. Sprinkle
with lemon juice and add enough stock or white wine and water
to come half way up the bulbs. Dot with butter, season, cover
with foil (shiny side down) and bake in the oven at 180°C
(350 °F, gas 4) for 1 hour, until the fennel is perfectly soft.

carottes vichy

The defining ingredients here are sugar and either bicarbonate of soda – known in France as Vichy salt – or Vichy water, a bottled water with a strong mineral flavour, much esteemed for health reasons. The French housewife doesn't like her vegetables undercooked and chewy: she likes them well-cooked and soft. She might, at the beginning of the season when the primeurs, the early baby vegetables, arrive in the market, choose not to cook the tender young things at all but present them as raw vegetables – crudités – and serve them as an hors d'œuvre with a mayonnaise. When cooked, green vegetables are usually steamed rather than boiled, drained as soon as they're soft, passed under the cold tap to halt the cooking process, then reheated as needed in generous amounts of butter.

Serves 4–6

1kg (2¼lb) young carrots, scraped and finely sliced
150ml (¼ pint) mineral water, preferably Vichy Saint-Yorre
1 teaspoon sugar
50g (2oz) unsalted butter
salt and freshly milled pepper
1 tablespoon chopped parsley

1 Put the sliced carrots into a heavy saucepan with the mineral water, sugar and a small piece of the butter – about the size of a hazelnut. Season with salt and pepper, bring to the boil and cover tightly.

2 Turn the heat right down and cook gently until all the liquid has been absorbed and the carrots are perfectly tender – 10–15 minutes. Remove the lid at the end of cooking and shake the pan over the heat to evaporate any remaining liquid.

3 Chop the remaining butter into small pieces. When you are ready to serve the carrots, toss them with the butter and parsley – both should retain their freshness.

eggs

œufs à la coque

SOFT-BOILED EGGS

If you do not have eggs from your own hens, choose free-range eggs from a reliable source. A perfectly soft-boiled egg is a fine-judged thing – down to a matter of seconds of cooking time. If the eggs have been refrigerated, allow them to come to room temperature before you start. In France, egg cups are not generally provided – you'll be expected to peel the eggs and eat them with a fork rather than slice off the top and eat the contents of the shell with a spoon.

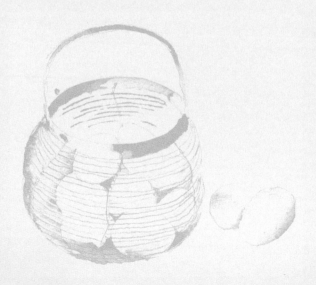

Serves 1

2 eggs

1 Bring a large saucepan of water to the boil. When it is boiling, remove it from the heat and slip in the eggs. Return the pan to the heat, cover and allow to simmer.

2 For a softly-set white and a runny yolk, remove the eggs with a draining spoon after 3–3½ minutes, depending on the size of the eggs. If you leave the eggs in the water for 1½ minutes longer, you will have oeufs mollets, hard-boiled eggs: plunge them immediately into cold water and then peel them, when you'll find the whites will be firm and the yolks still soft.

NOTE ~ The eggs are delicious salted and peppered as a dipping sauce for asparagus spears.

œufs en gelée

POACHED EGGS *in* ASPIC

This simple recipe depends on a well-flavoured aspic based on a strong consommé (see page 74), set either by the inclusion of a couple of veal knuckles or calf's foot in the basic broth, or with good-quality gelatine from a packet. Gelatine is available as crystals or as leaves – follow the instructions on the packet, making sure you soak the gelatine in cold water until it swells before you add it to the hot consommé, then mix well to blend thoroughly.

Serves 4

8 very fresh free-range eggs
2 tablespoons wine vinegar
2–3 fine slices ham, cut into thin strips
600ml (1 pint) aspic jelly, cooled to a soft set
8 small fresh tarragon sprigs or large leaves

1 Have ready eight little ramekins and a bowl of iced water. Crack one of the eggs into a cup. Bring 1 litre (1¾ pints) water to the boil in a roomy pan, such as a sauté pan or fairly deep frying pan. Add the vinegar (no salt as this will make the egg white separate) and bubble up again.

2 Turn the heat down so that the water simmers. Use a spoon to swirl the water into a whirlpool and slip in the egg from the cup, into the middle of the whirlpool. Prepare another in the same way and slip it in. Allow the eggs to poach for 3–4 minutes, keeping the water at a low simmer, then remove with a draining spoon and transfer to the iced water. Continue until all the eggs are cooked. Trim the eggs of any stray wisps of white.

3 Dip a few strips of ham in the aspic jelly and divide among the ramekins. Place a well-drained poached egg in each ramekin, surround with the remaining ham and top with a small sprig (or single large leaf) of tarragon. Cover the eggs with the aspic and transfer the ramekins to the fridge to set.

4 Unmould the eggs to serve or leave them in the ramekins. To unmould an egg, rinse a tea towel in very hot water and wrap it around the outside of the ramekin for a few seconds, remove the cloth and cover with a plate. Invert both ramekin and plate, then lift off the ramekin.

œufs pochés meurette

EGGS POACHED *in* RED WINE

I n this traditional recipe from the vineyards of Burgundy,
eggs poached in red wine take on a dramatically dark red
skin, veiling the white. The poaching liquid is then reduced to a
rich, shiny glaze without any additional thickening.

Serves 4

**1 bottle red Burgundy or any heavy red wine
8 fresh free-range eggs
8 small rounds day-old bread (the right size for a poached egg)
100g (4oz) unsalted butter, chilled
2 tablespoons diced lean bacon
2 tablespoons finely chopped shallot or onion**

1 Bring the wine to the boil in a roomy pan, such as a sauté pan or fairly deep frying pan. Reduce the heat so that the wine simmers. Break the eggs one by one into a cup and slip them into the simmering wine – cooking no more than two at a time is safest. Keep the wine simmering gently and allow 3–4 minutes cooking time. Remove each egg with a draining spoon as soon as the white has set and transfer it to a round of bread. Trim the egg to a neat shape and reserve.

2 In another pan, melt half the butter and fry the bacon and chopped shallot or onion for a few minutes – just long enough to soften (do not let them take colour).

3 Strain the poaching wine over the bacon mixture, bring to the boil and bubble fiercely for 15–20 minutes, until reduced by half.

4 Chop the chilled butter into small pieces. Remove the pan from the heat and gradually whisk in the bits of chilled butter to thicken the sauce and give it a shine.

5 Pour the sauce over the eggs. Do not worry if the eggs look a little grey – the sauce solves the problem. Serve immediately.

œufs brouillés aux truffes

SCRAMBLED EGGS *with* TRUFFLES

Egg shells, being porous, soak up the scent of a truffle like a sponge. So the canny truffle-hunter who intends to take his truffles to market next day buries them among a few fresh eggs overnight – one way to have your cake and eat it. Even better, though undeniably less profitable, is to scramble the eggs with the truffle.

Serves 4 as an hors d'œuvre

8 perfectly fresh free-range eggs
1 medium black truffle, about 50g (2oz) or larger is fine
50g (2oz) unsalted butter
salt and freshly milled pepper

TO FINISH
25g (1oz) unsalted butter, chilled and finely diced
fresh baguette or croutons fried in butter until crisp

1 Bury the truffle in the eggs overnight in a tightly covered jar. Next day, brush any soil off the truffle (do not rinse it unless this is really necessary) and cut it into fine matchstick slivers.

2 Crack the eggs into a bowl and fork them briefly to blend the yolk and white – do not beat them. Season with salt and pepper.

3 Melt the butter gently in a heavy pan without letting it brown. When it froths, add the truffle and toss it over the heat for 1 minute, no more.

4 Stir in the eggs and cook the mixture very gently, moving the base with a wooden spoon, until the eggs form creamy curds. Dot with the cold butter to halt the cooking process and serve immediately, with chunks of fresh baguette or croutons.

œufs en cocotte à la crème

BAKED EGGS *with* CREAM

For absolute authenticity, you need those little cocotte dishes with a single handle (ovenproof china, white on the inside, brown on the outside – very 1960s), though one-person soufflé dishes will do.

Serves 4 as a starter

8 very fresh free-range eggs
150ml (¼ pint) double cream
salt and freshly milled white pepper

1 Preheat the oven to 200°C (400°F, gas 6). Crack the eggs into eight ramekins or cocotte dishes (one egg per dish) or four individual soufflé dishes (two per dish). Drop a spoonful of cream in each dish and season lightly with salt and freshly milled white pepper. Do not butter the containers first or the egg will fry and harden instead of being tender and creamy.

2 Arrange the dishes in a bain-marie, a roasting tin with enough boiling water to come half way up the dishes. Bake for 6–8 minutes, until the eggs are softly set and still creamy. Serve without delay as the eggs continue to cook after they come out of the oven.

TESTING EGGS FOR FRESHNESS ~ To test an egg which lacks a date stamp for freshness, place it in a bowl of water (unsalted). If the egg remains horizontal and does not bob to the surface, it is perfectly fresh; if it tips towards the vertical and bobs upwards, it is not in the first flush of youth but is still edible; if it floats, it is really not worth eating. Floating has something to do with the presence or lack of air inside the shell: the shell, being porous, gradually allows the liquid-matter inside to evaporate, replacing it with air. A bad egg is unmistakable – the sulphurous smell is overwhelming.

tian de blea

BAKED CHARD OMELETTE

T he Provençal tian – a pastry-less quiche – takes its name from the shallow, round earthenware dish in which it is cooked. Unlike the omelette, however, cooked vegetables are always involved, the most characteristic being chard, beet-greens – drought-resistent spinach-like leaves, much-valued in the Mediterranean kitchen and particularly popular in the region of Nice where they take the place of all other greens. While the leaves are prepared like spinach, the fleshy white stalks are cooked separately and eaten like asparagus with an oil and vinegar dressing or an aïoli for dipping. In Old Nice, the chard tian is known as la trouchia and is sold, cut in thick wedges, in every cooked-food shop as a mid-morning snack.

Serves 4 as a main dish

750g (1lb 18oz) chard leaves (no stalks) or spinach, trimmed
2 tablespoons olive oil
1 garlic clove, crushed with a little salt
8 eggs
50g (2oz) strong cheese, such as Cantal or Parmesan, grated
½ teaspoon freshly grated nutmeg
salt and freshly milled pepper

1 Preheat the oven to 150°C (300°F, gas 2). Rinse the chard leaves thoroughly and shake dry. Drop them in a roomy saucepan with 1 tablespoon of the olive oil and the garlic crushed with a little salt. Cover tightly and shake over the heat for 4–5 minutes, until the leaves are wilted.

2 Transfer the chard to a sieve to drain. As soon as the greens are cool enough to handle, squeeze them thoroughly to extract as much moisture as possible. Chop them finely with a sharp knife.

3 Brush a 25cm (10in) tian or earthenware baking dish with a little of the remaining oil. Crack the eggs into a bowl and fork to blend the yolks and whites. Stir in the chopped leaves and grated cheese, season with nutmeg, salt and pepper and tip into the baking dish.

4 Transfer to the oven and bake for 35–40 minutes until just set – the tian will cook more as it cools. The low temperature allows the egg to set gently without bubbling. Serve warm or cool.

VARIATIONS ~ A fine tian can be made with a ragout of artichoke hearts. Allow one heart per egg and cook them gently until soft with a little white wine, olive oil and garlic.

Equally good is a tian made with a ratatouille (see page 46) or diced aubergines cooked in olive oil with plenty of sliced onion. The only rule is that the volume of vegetables should equal that of the eggs.

omelette aux fines herbes

HERB OMELETTE

You need a small frying pan, light enough to be easily tipped and kept solely for the purpose. Raw iron is traditional, non-stick the easier modern alternative. The size of the pan dictates the size of the omelette as the eggs take the shape of the pan. An 18–20cm (7–8in) pan is suitable for a 2–egg omelette to serve one person. For a 4–egg omelette to serve two, use a 22–24cm (8³/₄–9¹/₂in) diameter pan, and so on. The larger the pan, the larger the omelette. In the rural Languedoc, where my children attended school, on Shrove Tuesday (when all the eggs in the larder must be used up before Lent) their schoolmates made an omelette large enough to feed all the children in the village, cooking it in an enormous pan over an open fire in the woods. An omelette is served baveuse – frothy – never well-done. The traditional flavouring herbs are flat-leaf parsley, chives, chervil and tarragon. Make each omelette individually and serve it straight from the pan. The aim is a perfect little rolled bolster, soft in the middle and tenderly firm on the outside. For a filled omelette, omit the herbs and replace with a light stuffing, cooked in advance. Drop a spoonful of chopped mushrooms or tomatoes simmered in cream into the heart of the omelette before you flip it over. Or sprinkle with chopped ham or grated cheese.

Serves 1

**2 free-range eggs
a walnut-size piece of butter
1 tablespoon freshly chopped soft-leafed herbs
salt and freshly milled pepper**

1 Set a plate to warm before you begin. The omelette must be served as soon as it comes out of the pan.

2 Fork up the eggs with the herbs, a little salt and a generous turn of the pepper mill. The eggs should be frothy, but not thoroughly whisked.

3 Melt half the butter in a small omelette pan. The heat should be high, but not too high. When the butter foams but before it turns brown, roll it around the base and tip in the egg. Holding the handle with one hand and the fork with the other, move the eggs as they cook, drawing the set egg from the base of the pan in soft creamy curds, much as for scrambled eggs. After a moment, when the curds are just formed but still frothy, stop moving it so a skin can form on the base.

4 Drop the rest of the butter on the froth. Fold a third of the omelette over the middle third. Tip it out on to the warm plate, allowing the folded third to fold on to the open third to create a plump, oblong bolster. The omelette should be lightly browned on the outside but still juicy inside. The cooking should take no more than 1 minute – my tester says 30 seconds!

quiche lorraine

EGG AND BACON TART

This is the original quiche – an open-topped tart filled with a savoury custard – which takes its name from Germany's *kuchen*, the generic name for a cake. The original pastry base was a bread dough; the modern version is either shortcrust, as here, or puff pastry. I think it works best with shortcrust – not least because it is easy, quick and minimises the temptation to use ready-made. Home-made is really well worth the effort.

Serves 4

200g (7oz) plain flour
½ teaspoons salt
125g (4oz) unsalted butter, chilled
1 egg yolk

FILLING
250g (8oz) lean bacon or salted belly pork, finely diced
1 tablespoon butter
4 eggs, forked together
300ml (½ pint) double cream
¼ teaspoon freshly grated nutmeg
salt and freshly milled pepper

1 First make the pastry. Sift the flour into a bowl with the salt
and chop or grate in the chilled butter. Rub lightly between
your fingertips until the mixture looks like fine breadcrumbs.

2 Fork the egg yolk with 2 tablespoons very cold water. Still
using the tips of your fingers, work the yolk mixture into the
dry ingredients and press the mixture together to make a firm
ball of dough, adding a further 1 tablespoon water only if
necessary. Do not overwork. (You can make the pastry in a food
processor if you prefer.) Wrap the dough in cling film and set it
in a cool place for 30 minutes.

3 Preheat the oven to 200°C (400°F, gas 6). Have ready a
25cm (10in) round tart tin, preferably one with a removable
base. Tip the pastry-ball on to a floured board. With a floured

rolling pin, roll it out to a circle about 5mm (¼in) thick. Using the rolling pin to support the pastry, transfer it to the tart tin and ease it into the sides – do not stretch the pastry. Trim the pastry, leaving a rim of about 2.5cm (1in) to allow for shrinkage. Use trimmings to patch up any holes, pressing them in place with a damp finger.

4 Prick the pastry base with a fork in a few places and line with foil, shiny side down. Drop a few dried beans or rice-grains on the foil to keep it in place. Bake for 10 minutes to set the pastry. Remove the foil and bake for another 5 minutes to dry the surface. Leave to cool.

5 Meanwhile, gently fry the bacon or salted belly pork in the butter until the fat changes colour and begins to sizzle (do not let it brown). Leave to cool a little. Fork the eggs with the cream (do not beat), season with nutmeg, salt and pepper, and stir in the contents of the frying pan.

6 Tip the egg mixture into the cooled pastry shell, taking care not to overfill it or let the level come above the edge of the shell. Turn down the oven to 150°C (300°F, gas 2) and bake for 25–30 minutes, until the custard is lightly set and the pastry deliciously golden. Serve warm or at room temperature, never chilled.

Watch a French housewife as she makes her way slowly along the loaded stalls… searching for the peak of ripeness and flavour… What you are seeing is a true artist at work, patiently assembling all the materials of her craft, just as the painter squeezes oil colours onto his palette ready to create a masterpiece.

Keith Floyd

fish and shellfish

moules marinières

I n its simplest form, the freshly gathered mussels are opened in a closed pan over a heat sufficiently high for the shells to spring open immediately, discharging their liquid and providing the cooking liquor. Shop-bought mussels need a little extra assistance. Bivalves, such as mussels, can stay alive as long as they can hold water in their shells. To discover their condition, drop them in cold water, stir vigorously, watch closely and discard any that fail to close or remain shut. If in doubt, slide the two halves of the shell across each other: if the mussel is empty, the shells will slip open, revealing sand and debris inside. Mussels are a natural crop which need little or no husbandry. In the wild, they cling to rocks on the tide-line, feeding off whatever floats past. Farmed mussels are farmed only in the sense that the wild spat, free-range at this early stage, are encouraged to establish themselves on a particular support – a post or a rope. To prepare mussels for the pot, rinse thoroughly, scrub vigorously, and – finally, since the mussel won't last long without its beard – use a blunt knife to scrape off the whiskery little black tag which protrudes from the shell. Once bearded, the mussels lose water and must be cooked within the hour.

2kg (4½lb) mussels, scrubbed and bearded
50g (2oz) unsalted butter
1 tablespoon diced jambon cru (raw cured ham)
or lean bacon (optional)
2 shallots or 1 small onion, finely chopped
1 glass white wine

TO FINISH
chopped parsley/chopped garlic
freshly milled pepper

1 Rinse the mussels and discard any that do not shut when given a sharp tap.

2 Gently heat half the butter gently in a roomy pan. Add the ham or bacon and shallots or onion, and leave to fry for a moment to soften (do not let the ingredients brown).

3 Tip in the mussels and the wine, cover tightly and shake over the heat. The shells will pop open in the steam – stir to allow the ones at the top to drop to the bottom and feel the heat. When all the mussels have opened, they are done: remove the pan from the heat immediately (overcooked shellfish quickly toughen).

4 Finish with a little chopped parsley, garlic and pepper and ladle into bowls with their cooking broth. There is no need to add salt if you have included ham or bacon. Eat with your fingers – one shell can be used to scoop out the other.

VARIATIONS ~ For moules à la crème, strain the mussel broth, bubble up to reduce it by a third, and stir in its own volume of double cream, preferably the thick, slightly soured cream of Normandy. Bubble up again before pouring it back over the mussels. For extra richness, stir in a ladleful of béchamel sauce (see page 236).

For moules à la poulette, strain and bubble up the broth as above, stir in a couple of tablespoons of cream forked with 2 egg yolks. Heat gently in a bowl set over simmering water, whisking until the sauce thickens a little. Season with salt and freshly milled pepper, then pour the sauce back over the mussels (removed from their shells or left on the half-shell, as you please).

For moules frites, remove the mussel meat and marinate in lemon juice for 30 minutes, then dip in your favourite frying batter, and deep fry. Serve with quartered lemons.

Wherever you find mussels, you'll find sea-urchins. Prickly spheres the size of a golf-ball, these little sea-creatures are most commonly encountered when you get a clutch of their needle-like spikes stuck in your foot while exploring the rock-pools of the Mediterranean shoreline. By the time you manage to extract the creature's armoury, you'll probably never want to see it again. Which would be a pity because, once you manage to reach the edible parts, the prickly carapace hides one of the great delicacies of the Mediterranean table. Sea urchin corals (actually, the ovaries) are five little scraps of soft, fragrant caviar-flavoured flesh not much larger than a fingernail. Arranged in star-shape, these are only visible when the creature has been neatly sliced in half, a task which, since it's still alive and very prickly, is best left to those who know what they're doing. A wild-gathered crop, you'll find sea-urchins for sale in Mediterranean seaside markets from September to April. The seller will perform the service of opening the creatures for you. If not, use a protective glove and a pair of garden-clippers, or get yourself a coupe-oursin, specially designed scissors purchaseable in any French ironmongery. Once opened, the tender morsels won't last. You can eat them immediately with a squeeze of lemon, or wait till you get home and eat them folded at the last minute into softly scrambled eggs. Or make an oursinado: stir them into a little sauce of well-reduced white wine thickened with butter and egg yolks; eat with bread, or with poached eggs, or as a sauce for plain-poached fish.

huîtres au four

BAKED OYSTERS

The oyster farms of Brittany have been in business since
the days of the Romans, when the molluscs were sent
overland to the Empire's capital, packed in seaweed and tightly
barrelled (like all bivalves, they remain alive as long as they
can hold water in their shells). Here, their reputation as an
aphrodisiac made them in great demand at the feasts of
Saturnalia. In France, they remain the festive food of the
New Year, when they are sold by the lorry load. Neatly crated,
marked and priced by breed and size, the oysters are available
from supermarket forecourts throughout the land. For the
pleasure of contrast, serve a dozen chilled and a dozen grilled
oysters as a starter for a celebration supper.

Serves 2

12 oysters
4 tablespoons fresh breadcrumbs
2 tablespoons white wine or milk
4 tablespoons finely chopped shallots
1 tablespoon finely chopped parsley
salt and freshly milled pepper
100g (4oz) cheese, grated

1 Gripping the more cup-like of the shell halves firmly in a
cloth, open the oysters by levering the shells apart. This is
easiest to do with an oyster opener, a dagger-like instrument with
a protective hasp, although a short, strong knife will suffice if you
lack the purpose-made tool.

2 Preheat the oven to maximum, or heat the grill as high as
possible. Leaving each oyster on the deepest of its two shells,
arrange them in a shallow gratin dish in a single layer.

3 Soak the breadcrumbs briefly in the wine or milk to swell,
then mix in the chopped shallot and parsley. Season with salt
and freshly milled pepper and divide sparingly among the oysters
as a topping: the aim is to provide a crisp little hat, not a blanket.
Finish with a sprinkling of the grated cheese.

4 Slip the oysters into the top of a hot oven or under a grill and
allow 3–4 minutes cooking – just long enough to melt the
cheese and brown the breadcrumbs. Serve immediately.

tellines provençales

CLAMS IN TOMATO AND OLIVE SAUCE

I n Provence, the little purple-tinged clams known as tellines *are the preferred mollusk, although the larger palourdes, or any other bivalve, can be prepared in this way. Serve without reheating, as shellfish harden if overcooked.*

Serves 2 as a main dish, 4 as a starter

**2kg (4½lb) live shellfish (such as clams, mussels,
cockles, razor shells and queen scallops)
½ teaspoon saffron (about 12 strands)
4–6 tablespoons olive oil
1 large onion, finely chopped
3–4 garlic cloves, finely chopped
1.6kg (2¼lb) ripe tomatoes, peeled, seeded and diced
or canned are fine
1 bay leaf
1 sprig thyme
1 tablespoon pitted black olives, chopped
salt and freshly milled pepper
a little sugar
150ml (¼ pint) white wine**

TO FINISH
chopped parsley

1 Rinse the shellfish and leave them in a bucket of cold water for a few hours – overnight is best – to spit out their sand.

2 Toast the saffron in a dry pan for 1–2 minutes until it releases its scent – do not let it burn or it will be bitter. Transfer it to a cup containing a little boiling water. Leave to infuse for 15 minutes or so. This preliminary toasting of the saffron is a refinement supposedly to enhance the flavour – I am not entirely convinced, but try it for yourself.

3 Heat the olive oil in a roomy frying pan and fry the onion and garlic until soft and golden – do not let them brown. Add the tomatoes and bubble up, squashing the tomatoes down until they soften.

4 Add the bay leaf, thyme, olives, saffron with its soaking water and another glass of water. Bubble up again, then turn down the heat and leave to bubble for 20 minutes or so until the sauce is thick and rich.

5 Season with salt, pepper and a little sugar. Add the wine, bubble up again, and add the raw shellfish. Bubble up once more, cover loosely and let the shells open in the steam, shaking the pan every now and again to allow the top layer to drop to the bottom. Take the pan off the heat as soon as the shells gape open – 4–6 minutes, depending on the size of pan and thickness of the shells. Finish with plenty of chopped parsley.

coquilles st jacques sauce mornay

SCALLOPS *with* WINE AND CREAM

T he scallop, known as the pilgrim shell for its ability to propel itself through the water by means of a powerful adductor muscle, is a free-range bivalve – most shellfish are sedentary. It grows fine and sweet in the waters of the Atlantic. The curved shell, once emptied and scrubbed, is re-usable as a container for a little gratin of other fish: prawns, shrimp, diced fillets of sole or monkfish.

Serves 4

8–12 live scallops on the shell
300ml (½ pint) white wine
25g (1oz) butter
25g (1oz) plain flour
150ml (¼ pint) double cream
salt and freshly milled pepper
¼ teaspoon freshly grated nutmeg

TO FINISH
2 tablespoons chopped parsley
2 tablespoons fresh breadcrumbs
1–2 tablespoons melted butter

1 Rinse and scrub the scallops in their shells. To open, place them round-side down in a shallow pan with enough boiling water to come nearly to the top of the shells, set the pan on the heat and bring the water back to the boil. Alternatively, place the scallops in a roasting tin, add boiling water as in a pan, and transfer to a low oven. After a few moments the shells will open and you'll be able to lever a knife between the two halves, revealing the meat.

2 Remove the frill (the eyes) and the little sandy sack of intestine from the scallop. Slice the white adductor muscle horizontally into 2–3 medallions about 5mm (¼in) thick, and put them aside with the coral. Scrub the four largest curved shells and put them aside.

3 Preheat the grill. Bring the wine to the boil in a small pan. Slide in the white scallop meat and poach for 1½–2 minutes, just long enough for the fish to turn opaque. Remove and reserve. Add the corals to the pan, return the poaching liquid to the boil, cook for 1 minute, remove and reserve.

4 Melt the butter in a small pan until it foams, then sprinkle in the flour. Fry for 1 minute, then add the poaching liquid. Whisk over the heat until the sauce thickens. Then stir in the cream. Taste, season with salt, pepper and a pinch of nutmeg, and bubble up again.

5 Pour a little of the sauce into each of the four reserved scallop shells, top with the scallop meat and corals, and finish with the remaining sauce. Sprinkle with the chopped parsley and breadcrumbs, and trickle with a little melted butter. Slip under the grill to brown and bubble. Serve very hot.

bouillabaisse

FISH CHOWDER *with* SAFFRON

T he most famous of fish soups is one of those all-in
soup-stews served as two or even three courses that form
the entire meal. Its invention is attributed to the fish wives of
Marseilles and it takes its name, not (as so often with such
dishes) from the cooking implement, but from the method. A
bouillon-abaissé is a broth whose heat is raised and lowered and
then raised again, a process which encourages the broth to form
an emulsion with the oil. A dish that speaks to the heart as well

as the stomach, the bouillabaisse satisfies the emotional as well as the practical needs of the participants. As for the correct composition, it is not, in spite of what the chefs of the region will tell you, a recipe set in stone. Nonetheless some things are generally agreed. Extra-virgin olive oil should be used for the enrichment. Saffron is the only essential flavouring. Some fish are suitable, some are not. Shellfish are never included. For strength in the broth, there must be one or more of the rockfish – in France, these are rascasse, rouquier, labre, girelle, demoiselle. In addition to these, any collection of small fish sold as 'soup fish' will do with the exclusion of sardines, anchovies and all members of the flat fish family, including sole and turbot, any of which would make the broth bitter. Seven is the minimum number for which it is proper to prepare bouillabaisse, says the great 19th century authority on Provençal cooking, J–B Reboule. As for quantities, he suggests for sharing between two people, 1–1½kg (2¼–3¼lb) fish cooked in 1 litre (1¾ pints) water, plus 1 tablespoon olive oil per 500g (1lb 2oz) fish.

Serves 6–8 as a main course

4kg (8lb) of several different varieties such as:
rockfish of the wrasse family (rascasse)
sea bass (loup de mer)
monkfish (baudroie)
scorpion fish (chapon)
John Dory (saint-pierre)
conger eel
red mullet (rouget)
red gurnard (galinette)
whiting (merlan)
weever fish (vive)
spiny lobster (langouste, also known as crawfish, rock lobster)
shore crabs: stone, rock, green, blue, oyster or pea crab
and red crab
prawns, crayfish, shrimp
skate wings (raie)
escalopes or fillets of tuna, turbot, mackerel, bonito

THE BASIC BROTH
bones, heads, trimmings from the above,
including whole fish if small
3–4 shallots or leeks, chopped
3–4 garlic cloves, crushed
2 large tomatoes, peeled, seeded and chopped
3–4 sprigs each of fennel, parsley and thyme
a curl of dried orange peel
½ teaspoon saffron (about 12 strands)
salt and freshly milled pepper

**3–4 large, oval, yellow-fleshed potatoes, peeled
and quartered horizontally
about 8 tablespoons olive oil**

ROUILLE
**2 red peppers, whole or canned, prepared
4 garlic cloves
½ teaspoon salt
1 thick slice dry bread, about 50g (2oz)
2 red chillies, seeded and chopped**

TO FINISH
**4 dried bread rolls, sliced in half
(in Marseilles, navette a soupe)
1 garlic clove, halved**

1 Scale, trim and bone the fish as appropriate, reserving the heads and skeletons. Cut the larger fish into pieces roughly the same size as the smaller fish.

2 Divide the fish between two plates. Plate one should have firm fleshed fish, such as rascasse, weaver, gurnard, eel, monkfish, swordfish and anything else that feels firm to the finger, including any crustaceans. Plate two should have the soft-fleshed fish, such as sea bass, St. Peter's fish, whiting and whatever else that looks like a member of this group.

3 Put the fish debris, shallots or leeks, garlic, tomatoes, herb sprigs, orange peel and saffron in the cooking pot with 4 litres (7 pints) water. Bring to the boil, season with salt and

freshly milled pepper, turn down the heat and simmer for 20–30 minutes to extract all the flavour and body from the ingredients. Strain the broth and return it to the pot with the potatoes. Bring all back to the boil.

6 Meanwhile, make the rouille. Preheat the oven to 230°C (450°F, gas 8). Burn off the skin of the peppers by roasting them in the oven for about 15 minutes. Alternatively, burn them over a direct flame until the skin is charred. Place in a plastic bag to soften for 20 minutes, then separate the flesh from the skin with a knife.

5 Crush the garlic with the salt. Soak the bread in a little water and squeeze it dry. Pound the pepper flesh, garlic, bread and chillies to a smooth paste in a mortar with a pestle or in a food processor. Reserve.

6 Set a soup tureen and a large serving dish to warm along with sufficient soup plates. Tell all participants you will be ready to serve in exactly 10 minutes: as with the soufflé, the bouillabaisse waits for no man.

7 As soon as the broth and potatoes have come back to the boil, allow 10 minutes for the potatoes to soften a little. Add the firm-fleshed fish from plate one, starting with the crustaceans. Sprinkle with the olive oil, cover the pot again and bring all swiftly back to the boil. Boil rapidly for 5 minutes.

8 Lay the soft fish from plate two in the pot. Bring all swiftly back to the boil and continue boiling briskly, uncovered, for another 5 minutes.

9 Take the pot off the heat and, using a draining spoon, gently transfer the fish to the serving plate. Stir a ladleful of the hot fish broth into the rouille. Rub the bread rolls with a cut clove of garlic and spread with a little rouille (or hand this separately, as you please), and place the slices in the tureen. Ladle in a little of the broth and wait until the bread goes spongy – a minute or two.

10 Ladle in the rest of the broth. Set the tureen and the fish on the table at the same time. Provide a warm soup plate and a fork and spoon for each guest, along with a large napkin, fingerbowls and a communal plate for the little bones. Pass the rest of the rouille separately, with more bread, fresh this time, to accompany. Everyone eats as he or she pleases – soup with fish, soup then fish, anything goes. To accompany the bouillabaise, serve the good red wine of the Rhone valley and encourage your guests to drink up the last of the broth straight from the plate after the addition of a glass of wine – a gesture of appreciation known as faire chabrot.

NOTES ～ You may, if you wish, pass around a bowl of aïoli as well as the rouille. Although purists would reject the notion, it is worth it for the dramatic contrast between the fiery scarlet and the soft gold.

If all you have is a handful of bony little fish, make a bouillabaisse borgne – a strong fish broth, served with all its accompaniments, but with a handful of greens and a poached egg substituted for the larger chunks of fish in each portion.

The Corsican equivalent, *la zuminu*, includes squid, cuttlefish and whatever shellfish come to hand, such as mussels or clams, but lacks the saffron.

raie au beurre noir

SKATE *with* BLACK BUTTER

The nutty bitterness of the sharp little sauce perfectly complements the soft white strands of the skate meat which lie on the gelatinous bones and can be lifted off the skeleton like ribbons. It is a wonderful combination of texture, colour and flavour. Skate is the only fish that needs to be eaten two or three days after it has been caught, by which time the flesh will have ridden itself of the flavour of ammonia, a result of its natural response to stress.

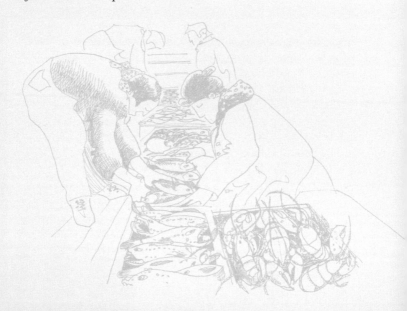

Serves 4

**1kg (2¼lb) skate wings
1 tablespoon white wine vinegar**

BLACK BUTTER
**125g (4½oz) unsalted butter
4 tablespoons chopped parsley
1 tablespoon red wine vinegar
salt and freshly milled pepper**

1 Bring the skate wings to the boil in plenty of well-salted water
  with the white wine vinegar added. Simmer for 10 minutes,
remove and drain.

2 Meanwhile, melt the butter in a small frying pan. Add the
  parsley. As soon as the parsley and the butter turn the colour
of mahogany, lift the pan from the heat. Count to ten and then
stir in the red wine vinegar. Without this pause, the hot butter
would spurt out of the pan as soon as the vinegar comes in
contact with it. Season with a little salt and freshly milled pepper.

3 Arrange the skate wings, dark side uppermost, on a warm
  serving dish and lift off the dark skin. The flesh slips easily
from the soft transparent bones. Serve with the black butter.

sole dieppoise

SOLE *with* CREAM AND SHRIMPS

The channel port of Dieppe has an in-shore fleet landing fish from the coasts of Picardy and Normandy. People drive over from Paris to meet the boats, competing with locals, scooping up the catch of shrimp, prawn and flat fish. Plaice or lemon sole can replace the sole, as long as they are perfectly fresh.

Serves 4

4 sole (2 if large), filleted and skinned
2 tablespoons flour, seasoned
50g (2oz) unsalted butter
about 150ml (¼ pint) white wine
150ml (¼ pint) double cream
1 tablespoon Pernod (optional)
salt and freshly milled white pepper
100g (4oz) raw shrimps or prawns, peeled or not

1 Flip the fish fillets in the seasoned flour to apply a light dusting, no more.

2 Melt half the butter in a large frying pan. When it foams, lay one or two fish fillets in the pan (or as many as fit without overlapping) and cook until opaque and firm, turning once, allowing 2–3 minutes on each side. Transfer to a warm plate or plates and keep hot while cooking the remaining fish.

3 Add the wine to the buttery residue in the pan and bubble up, scraping off any brown fishy bits. Bubble fiercely until the steam no longer smells of alcohol, and then whisk in the cream and remaining butter, cut into little pieces. Whisk in the Pernod (if using). Taste and season.

4 Slip in the shrimps or prawns and reheat gently. Do not let the sauce boil. The crustaceans will cook in a couple of minutes. Pour the sauce over the fish and finish with the shrimps or prawns.

SERVING SUGGESTION ~ As a main course, serve the sole in the French style, with vegetable accompaniments set on the table for people to help themselves. Plain white rice and braised fennel (see page 105) would be the perfect choice.

NOTE ~ Dover sole is skinned first and filleted afterwards, lemon sole should be filleted first, after which the fillets can easily be slipped off their skin with a sharp knife.

poultry

poulet au beurre

BUTTER-ROAST CHICKEN

Choose an organic free-range bird for this simple but perfect way with the Sunday chicken. French cooks value flavour and texture over size and plumpness in their poultry, enthusiastically discussing provenance and virtues of each breed, weighing up the merits of the blue-legged chickens of Bresse against those of the succulent chickens of the Landes. In this recipe, a protective coating of herb butter between the skin and the breast keeps the white meat perfectly moist, while the bird is regularly turned to ensure a crisp, buttery skin.

Serves 4–6

2kg (4¼lb) chicken with giblets
sea salt and freshly milled black pepper
1 unwaxed lemon
2–3 fresh thyme sprigs
75g (3oz) unsalted butter
3 tablespoons finely chopped fresh tarragon

1 Preheat the oven to 220°C (425°F, gas 7). Wipe the chicken inside and out and season the cavity generously with salt and pepper. Soften the lemon by rolling it back and forth on a flat surface, and prick it all over with a fork. Tuck the giblets, lemon and thyme in the cavity.

2 Mash 50g (2oz) of the butter with the tarragon and ½ teaspoon each of salt and pepper. Starting at the neck end of the chicken, work your fingers over one side of the breast meat between the flesh and skin – be gentle as the skin is fragile. Repeat down the other side.

3 Working on the outside, press the skin to even out the butter, patting the skin back into place. Spread the remaining butter over the chicken, and season.

4 Settle the bird on its side on a rack in a roasting tin. Roast for 20 minutes. Turn it carefully, taking care not to break the skin, and roast on the other side for another 20 minutes. Turn the chicken on to its back, breast up, and roast for another 20 minutes, until the bird is deeply bronzed all over.

5 Reduce the heat to 190°C (375°F, gas 5) and turn the chicken breast-side down – try to set it at an angle such that the tail is in the air. Roast for about another 15 minutes, until the juices from the thigh run clear when the meat is pierced with a skewer. No need to baste.

6 Transfer the bird to a warm serving dish, still with its tail in the air, and cover loosely with foil. Let it rest in a turned-off oven (leave the door ajar) for at least 10 minutes – 30 minutes is fine. The bird will continue to cook while the meat firms up and the juices are re-absorbed.

7 Carve the chicken in the kitchen and dish it up in its glory. The French never carve at table. Hand around a bowl of undressed salad leaves, such as frisée, mâche and watercress; the buttery juices are the only dressing needed.

poulet au riz

CHICKEN *with* RICE

This is a delicate dish that depends on long gentle cooking. A roasting fowl will do, though the broth will be stronger if the bird is an elderly barnyard hen, and the head, neck and feet (scalded and scrubbed) are included.

Serves 4–6

1 free-range chicken, about 2kg (4½lb), or a mature boiling fowl
2–3 carrots, cut into chunks
3–4 celery sticks, chopped
1 onion, stuck with 2 cloves
a small bunch of parsley, marjoram, thyme and a bay leaf
finely grated zest and juice of 1 lemon
½ teaspoon white peppercorns
1 litre (1¾ pints) veal or chicken stock
250g (8oz) round-grain rice, such as Camargue, risotto or paella
125g (4½oz) unsalted butter
1 tablespoon plain flour
finely grated zest and juice of ½ lemon
¼ teaspoon grated nutmeg
150g (¼ pint) double cream
1 heaped tablespoon finely chopped parsley
salt and freshly milled pepper

1 Wipe the bird inside and out. Place it in a roomy pot, pack the sides with the carrots, celery, onion, herbs, half the lemon zest and juice, peppercorns and salt. Add the stock and enough water to submerge the ingredients completely.

2 Bring to the boil, cover the pot and turn down the heat so that the stock simmers. Leave to cook gently for 1½–2 hours, without allowing any large bubbles to break the surface, until the bird is perfectly tender. If you are using a boiling-fowl, allow 2½–3 hours.

2 Rinse the rice in a sieve or fine colander under the cold tap until the water runs clear, then transfer to a saucepan. Add enough cold water to cover generously, bring to the boil and cook for 5 minutes, stirring to avoid sticking. Tip the rice back into the sieve or colander and rinse under warm water to wash away the stickiness of the starch.

3 Return the rice to the pan and add 600ml (1 pint) of the hot chicken broth from the pot. Bring the rice to the boil, add 25g (1oz) of the butter, turn down the heat and cook gently for 15–18 minutes, until the grains are perfectly tender. Fork over the rice and add another knob of the butter – the grains should be separate but not dry.

4 Meanwhile make the sauce. Melt another 25g (1oz) butter in a small pan. As soon as it foams, sprinkle in the flour, cook very gently for 3–4 minutes until the mixture looks sandy but do not let it brown. Whisk in 600ml (1 pint) of the hot chicken broth, bubble up, turn down the heat and simmer gently for 10 minutes.

5 Season the sauce with 1 tablespoon of the remaining lemon juice, a pinch of the finely grated zest and the nutmeg. Bubble up again and whisk over the heat until reduced by a third. Stir in the cream and the remaining butter cut into small pieces and reheat, whisking throughout, until boiling. Taste and add salt and pepper if needed.

6 To serve, heap the rice on an oval serving dish and top with the chicken, skinned and jointed. Finish with a ladleful of the sauce and a shower of finely chopped parsley. Hand the rest of the sauce separately.

VARIATIONS ~ For poulet en demi-deuil, literally chicken in half-mourning, slip thin slices of fresh black truffle between the skin and the flesh of the chicken (for perfection, the bird should be entirely covered in truffle) and poach as in the main recipe.

coq au vin

CHICKEN IN RED WINE

An ancient recipe from the Auvergne, this is traditionally made with a sinewy barnyard cockerel simmered in the robust red wine of the region – a Chambertin or Mâcon. A rooster is a lean, muscular bird that needs long gentle cooking to tenderise it. A roasting fowl will will only need an hour.

Serves 4

1 free-range chicken, about 2kg (4½lb),
jointed, with the back and giblets
salt and freshly milled pepper
1 tablespoon unsalted butter
100g (4oz) streaky bacon, diced
500g (1lb 2oz) small shallots or baby onions, peeled but whole
250g (9oz) morels or button mushrooms
2 tablespoons brandy or marc
1 garlic clove, crushed with a little salt
1 bottle robust red wine
a small bunch of thyme, parsley and a bay leaf

BEURRE MANIE
1 tablespoon unsalted butter
1 tablespoon plain flour

1 Trim the chicken joints of any excess fat, but do not skin them. Season with salt and pepper and set aside.

2 Melt half the butter in a roomy casserole and fry the bacon and shallots or onions until lightly browned, then remove and reserve. Add the morels or button mushrooms, sprinkle with a little salt, and let them fry in the hot juices for a few minutes, then remove and add them to the reserved onions.

3 Melt the remaining butter in the pot and add the chicken joints. Fry them until they take a little colour, then sprinkle with the brandy and set it alight to burn off the alcohol and caramelise the chicken skin a little.

4 Add the garlic and red wine, and bubble up. Return the reserved onions, bacon and mushrooms to the pot, season with salt and pepper, and tuck in the herbs. Bring back to the boil, turn down the heat and cover tightly. Leave to simmer gently for 1–1½ hours, until the chicken is perfectly tender.

5 Work the butter to a smooth paste with the flour to make the beurre manie. Remove the herbs and transfer the chicken joints to a warm serving dish with the mushrooms and onions. Return the pot to the heat, bubble up the juices and whisk in the beurre manie. Bubble the sauce up for a few minutes until it is smooth, glossy and no longer tastes of raw flour.

6 Pour the sauce over the chicken. Serve with potatoes mashed with hot milk and unsalted butter, or – country-style – with thick slices of country bread for mopping the juices. Accompany with the same robust red wine that served as the cooking broth.

suprême de volaille aux morilles

BREAST OF CHICKEN *with* MOREL MUSHROOMS

T he tender white breast meat on a chicken is known as the
suprême, one on each side of the breast bone. A French
cook would expect to buy the whole bird and have the butcher
prepare the suprêmes as required – skinned or not, with or
without a hank of wing-bone. The carcasses would then provide
the basis for a fine strong stock, the meat picked from the bones
and folded into a béchamel sauce as the filling for a vol-au-
vent ordered from the pâtisserie.

Serves 4

4 chicken breasts
2 tablespoons plain flour, seasoned
100g (4oz) fresh morels or 50g (2oz) dried morels, soaked
50g (2oz) unsalted butter
150ml (¼ pint) white wine
about 150ml (¼ pint) double cream
pinch of sugar (optional)
salt and freshly milled pepper

1 Wipe the chicken breasts and flip them over in the seasoned flour. Carefully clean the fresh morels: do not rinse the caps but use a brush to get the sand out of the wrinkles; trim the bases as they are inclined to be woody. Drain soaked dried morels and reserve the soaking liquid.

2 Melt the butter in a roomy frying pan. As soon as it foams, lay the chicken breasts in the pan. Fry gently, turning once, for 5 minutes or so, until the meat begins to firm up.

3 Add the morels (if soaked, include the reserved soaking water) and wine and bubble up. Turn down the heat, cover the pan loosely and simmer gently for 10–15 minutes, until the alcohol has evaporated and the breasts are firm.

4 Remove the lid and bubble up to reduce the juices to a couple of spoonfuls. Stir in the cream and check the seasoning (adding a little sugar, perhaps?). Bubble up again to amalgamate the cream with the wine sauce. Transfer everything to a warm serving dish. Simple, really.

NOTE ~ The chicken is good with a puree of celeriac and potato spiced with a little nutmeg.

Other wild mushrooms can replace the morels: chanterelles, pieds de mouton, trompettes de la mort; cultivated oyster mushrooms and button mushrooms are also suitable.

chaud-froid de poulet

POACHED CHICKEN SALAD

An exquisite dish whose excellence depends on perfect raw materials. A free-range chicken is poached, allowed to cool in its own juices and then dressed with home-made lemon mayonnaise enriched with a reduction of the cooking broth. There is absolutely no need for fancy garnishings – just let the flavour of the dish tell its own story.

Serves 4–6

1 small free-range chicken
1 small onion, quartered
2–3 celery tops
1 leek, cut into chunks
1 teaspoon allspice berries
½ teaspoon white peppercorns
1 teaspoon salt

MAYONNAISE
2 egg yolks
finely grated zest and juice of 1 lemon
1 teaspoon mild French mustard (tarragon mustard is good)
about 450ml (¾ pint) light olive oil or half olive oil
and half sunflower oil
salt and freshly milled white pepper

TO SERVE
crisp hot bread rolls
quartered lettuce hearts
tomato salad

1 Remove any extraneous fat from inside the chicken. Settle the bird, breast uppermost, in a roomy pot that will just accommodate it, and pour in enough cold water to submerge it completely. Bring to the boil and skim off any grey foam that rises to the surface.

2 Add the onion, celery tops, leek, allspice, peppercorns and salt. Bring back to the boil, turn down the heat so that the water simmers gently and cover the pan. Poach the chicken delicately for about 1 hour without letting it boil, adding more hot water if necessary. The French say the liquid should smile. If you prefer, transfer the pan to the oven once the liquid has boiled, and leave it to simmer at 170°C (325°F, gas 3). The chicken is done when the thigh waggles easily in the socket.

3 Let the chicken cool for 30 minutes in its cooking broth. Remove, skin and strip all the meat from the bones; do not forget the little oysters (two small round nuggets of meat) from the back. Transfer the meat to a bowl, pour in a couple of ladlefuls of broth and place in the fridge for the chicken to drink its juices – overnight is best, but 4–5 hours will do. Reserve the broth and keep it in the fridge.

4 Remove the chicken pieces from their jelly and cut them into bite-sized strips – the meat will be deliciously moist and gelatinous. Lift off the hat of white fat on the excess jelly and the reserved jellied broth (it is lovely for frying potatoes) and tip both into a pan. Boil the broth down until it is reduced to about 150ml (¼ pint).

5 Leave the broth to cool while you make the mayonnaise. When you begin, all ingredients should be at room temperature. Put the egg yolks in a bowl with 1 teaspoon of the lemon juice and the mustard. Blend quickly with a wire whisk, then whisk in the oil, adding it very slowly at first. Steadily increase the stream of oil as the mayonnaise thickens, working in more lemon juice – not too much, just enough to sharpen the mayonnaise.

6 As soon as the mayonnaise starts to thicken it is easier to switch to a wooden spoon. You may need more or less oil, depending on the weather and the size of the yolks, but the mixture should be about the consistency of soft butter. Beat in enough of the cooled chicken stock to dilute the mayonnaise to a coating consistency. Stir in the lemon zest, taste and season.

7 Combine the shredded chicken with the mayonnaise and serve with hot crisp rolls, quartered lettuce hearts and a little salad of chopped peeled tomatoes dressed with a pinch of sugar.

pintade farcie aux pommes

STUFFED GUINEA FOWL *with* APPLES

This sumptuous party dish comes from Normandy, land of Calvados and cream. The apples in the stuffing impart a flowery fragrance to the gamey little guinea fowl, while the gentle braising keeps them juicy. Guinea fowl, an African native, is comparatively recently domesticated and, although it is a popular barnyard bird in rural France, it has retained the muscular leanness of its wild ancestor. Four partridges, a brace of pheasant or 2 small free-range chickens are the alternatives.

Serves 6

2 guinea fowl
1 onion, finely chopped
50g (2oz) butter
150g (5oz) minced pork
150g (5oz) minced beef
6 yellow-fleshed apples, such as Reinettes or Golden Delicious
1 small glass Calvados or brandy
1 egg, forked to blend
salt and pepper
1 teaspoon dried thyme

TO FINISH
6 tablespoons crème fraîche or double cream soured with
a little lemon juice
1 tablespoon butter for frying

1 Preheat the oven to 200°C (400°F, gas 6). Wipe the birds inside and out, and singe off any stray little hairs or feathers by turning them quickly over a gas flame. (Or use long matches to singe off the hairs.)

2 For the stuffing, fry the onion in half the butter. Add the pork and beef, and fry gently until the meats change colour.

3 Peel and dice 2 of the apples, and add them to the pan. Sprinkle with the Calvados or brandy and cover loosely. Leave to stew gently for 15–20 minutes, until the apple pieces have softened but have not quite lost their shape. Season with salt

and pepper, remove from the heat and let the mixture cool a little before you work in the egg.

4 Divide the stuffing between the birds, spooning it into their body cavities. Tie their drumsticks together with thread to keep them neatly in shape. Transfer the stuffed birds to a roasting tin, breasts downwards. Dot with the remaining butter, add a sprinkle of thyme, and salt and pepper.

5 Roast the birds at the high heat for the first 10 minutes. Turn the birds breast side up, dot with a little more butter, and cover with foil, shiny side down. Reduce the heat to 150°C (300°F, gas 2) so that the birds cook slowly and make plenty of juice. Cook for about 1 hour, until the birds are perfectly tender and the drumsticks pull easily away from the body.

6 Remove from the oven and leave to rest for 10 minutes. Quarter the birds and pile the stuffing up in the middle of a warm serving dish. Tip the pan juices into a small saucepan, skim off the oily slick of butter from the top and reserve.

7 Reheat the juices and bubble up fiercely for 3–4 minutes to reduce them to a strong sticky gravy. Stir in the crème fraîche or cream, taste, season with salt and pepper and reheat without boiling to make a little sauce.

8 Meanwhile peel, quarter and core the rest of the apples. Sauté them in the reserved butter until they brown a little, taking care they do not lose their shape (you may need extra butter).

9 Arrange the apple quarters on the stuffing and pile the quartered birds on top. Trickle with a little of the sauce and hand the rest of the sauce separately.

caneton à la bigarade

DUCKLING *with* ORANGE

A dish for winter, when the ducklings are well grown and bitter oranges, bigarades – otherwise known as marmalade or Seville oranges – are in season. Choose unwaxed fruit or scrub them thoroughly to remove the coating. A duck carcass weighs heavy and the meat to bone ratio is not as favourable as it is with other birds, so allow 600g (1lb 5oz) per person.

Serves 4

1 well-grown duckling, about 2kg (4½lb) dressed weight
25g (1oz) unsalted butter
salt and freshly milled pepper

TO FINISH
3 bitter oranges or 2 sweet oranges plus the juice of 1 lemon
1 heaped tablespoon caster sugar
2 tablespoons chicken or veal stock
50g (2oz) butter, chilled and chopped small

1 Preheat the oven to 160°C (325°F, gas 3). Rub the duckling inside and out with salt and pepper and truss it neatly. Melt the butter in a heavy flameproof casserole and brown the bird all over.

2 Cover tightly and cook in the oven for 25–30 minutes. Alternatively, cook over low heat, turning the bird regularly to avoid burning. Remove from the heat when the juices spooned from the cavity are a clear pink – a duck should always be slightly undercooked and the breast meat should be rosy rather than grey or the bird will be tough.

3 Meanwhile, finely pare the zest from the oranges and cut it into fine strips or use a zester to remove the zest in strands. Pare and discard the pith from the flesh and carve out the segments, leaving the membranes behind and squeezing the juice into a bowl. Reserve the zest, juice and segments (discard the pips).

4 When the duck is perfectly roasted, transfer it to a hot serving dish and surround with the orange segments. Pour off the excess fat, reserve the cooking juices in the casserole, setting it aside.

5 Place the sugar in a small, heavy-bottom saucepan and heat gently until it melts and caramelises lightly – you are looking for a pale golden brown. Add the lemon juice (if using) and remove from the heat. Stir in the stock and the reserved orange zest and juice, return to the heat and bubble up.

6 Add the orange mixture to the drippings in the pan and bubble up again, scraping the base to include all the sticky brown bits. Strain the sauce, taste and season. Reheat to boiling and whisk in the butter to thicken the sauce and give it a shine.

7 Carve the duck before you take it to table, and coat the joints with the sauce.

VARIATIONS ~ For caneton au navets – duck with turnips – prepare the duckling as above, omitting the oranges, and serve with baby turnips caramelised in butter with a little sugar and finished in the duck juices.

For caneton au petits pois – duck with peas – prepare the duck as above, omitting the oranges. Cook freshly shelled peas in the duck juices; finish with bits of chilled butter to add thickness and shine.

For caneton aux olives – duck with olives – cook the duck as above, omitting the oranges. Finish the juices with green olives (scald them first to remove excess salt) and a few flakes of chilled butter.

magrets de canard poêlés

SEARED DUCK BREASTS

The simplest way to ensure that the choicest morsel of the bird, the breast meat, remains tender and juicy is to cook it very briefly over a high heat, and then let it rest and firm up. The French have a choice of two breeds of domestic duck. The Nantais – named for the town of Nantes – is the smaller and weighs around 1.5kg (3¼lb), while the Rouennais – after the town of Rouen – weighs well over 2kg (4½lb). The Rouennais is not bled during slaughter, a method that produces much darker meat which, though delicious when cooked rare and pink, is more vulnerable to spoilage. Buy the whole duck, lift the breasts off the bone with a sharp knife, and make a pâté with the carcass and legs.

∞

Serves 2

2 duck breasts, boned
salt and freshly milled pepper

1 Lightly score the duck skin without cutting through to the flesh. Season the meat on both sides.

2 Heat a heavy iron pan until smoking. Place the duck breasts skin sides down on the hot metal and cook for 3–4 minutes, until the fat softens and begins to run, and the skin gilds.

3 Turn the duck breasts carefully and sear them on the other side, allowing another 2–3 minutes. Remove the pan from the heat and leave on the side of the stove for 5 minutes for the meat to firm up and settle. Test for doneness by prodding with your index finger: very rare meat feels soft and spongy; if the meat feels hard, it's overdone (unlikely at this point). If the duck breasts are still soft, set the oven at 160°C (325°F, gas 3) and transfer them to the oven for 10 minutes. Duck breast should be quite pink, almost bloody. To serve, slice them on the diagonal.

SERVING SUGGESTIONS ~ Serve with pommes de terre salardais (see page 96/97). Alternatively, boil potatoes, slice them while they are still hot and sauté them in goose fat. They are ready when they are golden brown and flecked with little crisp bits. For absolute perfection, include a few slivers of black Perigord truffle.

You can, if you wish to, make a little sauce to go with the duck. Deglaze the pan with a splash of Armagnac and stir in some cream or boil up a glass of red wine with the pan drippings and finish with a knob of cold butter.

garbure béarnaise

SLOW-COOKED VEGETABLES *with* GOOSE CONFIT

The garbure, the traditional rural midday meal of southern France, is at its most sumptuous in the kitchens of Béarn. At its simplest, it is a meatless vegetarian hot-pot much like Italy's minestrone. But in Béarn it always includes a joint or two of confit, fattened goose or duck preserved in its own dripping. Traditionally, it was sent to the breadmaker's oven, a service once provided by the village baker. The basic ingredients are variable, depending on season and regional preference: in Provence, a ratatouille layer is usual; in the Languedoc in spring, green vegetables and potatoes replace the beans and cabbage. You can replace the confit with pork chops or omit the meat altogether.

Serves 4 as a main dish

**8 thick slices country bread
500g (1lb 2oz) onions
8 tablespoons olive oil
1–2 bay leaves
4 tablespoons chopped mixed parsley, chervil and marjoram
2–3 garlic cloves, chopped
salt and freshly milled pepper
4–5 large tomatoes, peeled and chopped
4 tablespoons cooked haricot beans
2 leg joints of goose or duck confit (see page 181)
1 large chunk pumpkin or butternut squash, peeled and sliced
½ green cabbage, shredded
grated cheese to finish (optional)**

TO SERVE
**green salad
pickled gherkins and capers**

1 Preheat the oven to 170°C (325°F, gas 3). Slice the bread and put it to dry and crisp for 10 minutes or so while the oven heats up.

2 Meanwhile, fry the onions gently in 3 tablespoons of the olive oil until soft and golden – do not let them brown further.

3 Now you are ready to assemble the garbure. Spread half the onion in a layer in the base of a roomy casserole. Top with half the dried bread. Season with bay, chopped herbs, garlic, and

salt and pepper. Top with layers of tomatoes, beans, confit, pumpkin and a handful of the shredded cabbage, seasoning between the layers each time.

4 Repeat the layering in the same order, finishing with the remaining bread. Pour in a tumbler of water and trickle with the rest of the oil.

5 Cover tightly and bake for about 1½–2 hours, until everything is deliciously tender. Turn the oven down a notch after the first hour and check if you need to add a little more water. Take the cover off for the last 15 minutes, sprinkle with a thick layer of grated cheese (if using), and turn the oven up to crisp the top.

6 To serve, scoop through the layers and ladle the garbure into deep soup plates. Offer a green salad and pickles (gherkins, capers) on the side. You will need a carafe of red wine for the goudale, the term for a glass of wine poured into the last of the broth and drunk straight from the plate. Very rustic.

Cuisine is when things taste like themselves....In cooking, as in all the arts, simplicity is the sign of perfection.

Curnonsky

cassoulet de castelnaudary

BEANS BAKED *with* GOOSE CONFIT

The cassoulet of Castelnaudary, according to the inhabitants of the windswept town in the Languedoc where my children attended school, is the only true version of this stupendous beanpot. And who am I argue? In Toulouse or Carcassonne, they might add mutton or lamb, some might even include a brace of partridges, but Madame Escrieux (my neighbour, whose recipe this is) would have none of these. The Escrieux family, subsistence farmers with the right to operate their own still, potted their own confit, grew their own beans (though the beans of Soissons were held acceptable) and kept and slaughtered their own pig. The dish was reserved for the winter months and only eaten at midday on Sunday, since it needed a full day and a night to digest.

Serves 6–8

FIRST COOKING
1kg (2¼lb) white haricot beans
1 whole head garlic
500g (1lb 2oz) belly pork
2 large carrots, cut into chunks
1 onion, stuck with 6 cloves
a small bunch of parsley, thyme, rosemary and bay
½ teaspoon cracked black pepper

SECOND COOKING
1–2 joints of goose or duck confit (see page 181)
500g (1lb 2oz) lean pork, cut into bite-sized chunks
3 garlic cloves, crushed
1 onion, chopped
500g (1lb 2oz) tomatoes, peeled and chopped (canned are fine)
500g (1lb 2oz) fresh all-meat pork sausage,
such as saucisson de Toulouse
4 tablespoons goose fat from the confit, melted
salt and freshly milled pepper

TO FINISH
2–3 tablespoons fresh breadcrumbs

1 Soak the beans overnight in cold water. Drain and transfer to a large cooking pot – a toupin is the correct container. For a charred, lightly caramelised flavour, turn the head of garlic over in a gas flame

2 Remove the skin from the belly pork and tie it up in a neat roll; dice the pork. Add the meat and roll of skin to the beans in the pot with all the other ingredients for the first cooking: the garlic, carrots, onion, herbs and pepper. Cover all the ingredients generously with fresh water, bring to the boil, and skim off the grey foam which rises. Boil for 10 minutes. Then turn down the heat and simmer the beans for 1 hour, or until they are soft but still whole, adding more boiling water if necessary.

3 Meanwhile, prepare the ingredients for the second cooking. Warm the joints of goose or duck confit in a roomy frying pan until the fat runs, then remove and reserve the meat. Fry the pork with the garlic in the drippings, until all the pieces are browned. Remove and reserve both meat and garlic. Fry the onion in the drippings until soft and golden.

4 Preheat the oven to 150°C (300°F, gas 2). When the beans are ready, take out the garlic, onion and the herbs. Remove and untie the roll of pork skin and lay it in the base of a roomy casserole, fat downwards. Drain the beans, reserving the cooking liquor. Layer half the beans in the casserole with the meats, onions, tomatoes and sausage. Finish with the rest of the beans. Pour in the reserved cooking liquor to cover the ingredients. Cover the pot.

5 Transfer to the oven and leave to cook gently for about 2 hours. If the beans get too dry, pour in a little boiling water (the beans will harden if you use cold water).

6 Trickle a tablespoonful of the melted goose fat over the beans. Increase the oven heat to 160°C (325°F, gas 3) and return the pot, uncovered, to the oven. It will take 30 minutes to form a

beautiful crust. Break it with a spoon and stir it into the beans once more. Sprinkle with the breadcrumbs and trickle with another tablespoonful of goose fat.

7 Return the casserole to the oven for 30 minutes, then break the crust again and stir it in. Trickle with the remaining goose fat. Leave for the final 30 minutes. Now you reap the reward of your patience: beneath the golden crust the meats will be tender and fragrant, and the beans melted into a delicious creamy mass.

MAKING DUCK OR GOOSE CONFIT ~ To make your own confit, choose a large pottery or stoneware ovenproof jar or pot and drop in as many duck or goose joints as will comfortably fit. Season with salt, peppercorns, a bay leaf and juniper berries. Melt the contents of a tin of gras d'oie (available from the supermarket deli section) and pour in enough to completely submerge the duck joints. Heat the oven to the lowest possible setting and leave the duck or goose in the oven overnight. That's all.

To use, melt gently and remove the joints. The confit is delicious as the star ingredient of a warm salad; the fat makes exquisitely crisp sauté potatoes that are terrific with a few wild mushrooms, maybe the first of the year's chanterelles.

game

marcassin en daube

SLOW-COOKED WILD BOAR

To flavour a daube, the cooks of Provence like to use dried orange zest, and the common variety of thyme is replaced by serpolet, a highly aromatic wild member of the same family. The daubière is the closed earthenware pot in which stews are traditionally simmered.

Serves 6

1.5kg (3½lb) wild boar meat, diced
2 tablespoons plain flour, seasoned
4–5 tablespoons olive oil
8 garlic cloves, in their skins
2 tablespoons diced streaky bacon
3 large tomatoes, peeled and chopped
1–2 sprigs serpolet or thyme
1 curl orange zest, preferably dried, but fresh is fine
1 glass white wine
600ml (1 pint) stock

TO FINISH
100g (4oz) mushrooms
1 tablespoon olive oil
4 salted anchovies
50g (2oz) black olives, chopped
salt and freshly milled pepper

1 Dust the meat in the seasoned flour and fry in the olive oil until it browns a little. Wild meat is drier and firmer than farmed meat, so it takes less time to caramelise. Remove and reserve.

2 Add the whole unskinned garlic cloves and the bacon to the pan drippings and fry for a few minutes. Add the tomatoes, serpolet or thyme and orange zest and bubble up, squashing the tomatoes down until they collapse.

3 Pour in the wine and the stock and bubble up again. Return the meat to the pan and add seasoning. Turn down the heat, cover the pan loosely and leave to simmer gently, for as long as it takes for the meat to be so tender it can be eaten with a fork – about 2–3 hours – add a little water if necessary

4 When the meat is nearly done, fry the mushrooms in the oil in a small frying pan. Add the anchovies and mash them into the mushrooms so they melt in the hot juices. Add the olives and heat for 1–2 minutes. Stir this aromatic mixture into the stew 5 minutes before the end of cooking.

SERVING SUGGESTION ~ Serve with white rice or fresh noodles, lightly buttered, and rough country bread rubbed with garlic.

Wild boar, marcassin, is the most prized of the huntsman's bag and is still to be found in the mountainous and forested areas of France where cultivation is impractical or which were formerly reserved as the king's hunting forest. Following the implementation of the Code Napoleon (the basis of French laws, particularly those of inheritance) possessions had to be divided equally among all recognised heirs, reversing the law of inheritance by first born and turning France into a nation of small farmers. The result was that most land fell into the hands of subsistence farmers. These days even the most urban French citizen considers himself a countryman, possessed of a stake in a patch of scrub which, however small, can be viewed as his personal hunting territory; a change from the days when the produce of the king's hunting forest was reserved for the royal table.

Wild meat is noticeably leaner, darker and more sinewy than the domesticated equivalent; it takes best to long slow cooking in a daube or as the basis for a country pâté. Recipes for wild meat usually include additional fat, for example from belly pork or bacon, to counter the natural leanness and help to tenderise the meat, rather than allowing it to remain chewy. Wine, particularly when used as a marinade, enhances the gamey flavour, though the alcohol must always be evaporated during cooking.

Flavouring herbs, particularly rosemary, thyme, oregano, juniper and wild garlic, are chosen to reflect the diet available in the wild, when they are consumed in the form of young shoots, berries or roots. When cooking game, a touch of romance – preferably the huntsman's own description of the chase – is as much a part of the recipe as the ingredients.

Even in highly cultivated areas, the Frenchman is so devoted to the possibilities of la chasse that patches of woodland and scrub are left as shelter for small game – hare, rabbits, partridge, pheasant – and as gathering patches for wild fungi and fruits.

Although a boar is the most prized of the hunter's bag – a quarry admired as much for the danger of the pursuit as for the excellence of the meat – venison and hare are also valued, and recipes for one or the other are interchangeable. Rabbit is the poor man's meat, is usually trapped rather than hunted, and is not protected by a closed season. Of the feathered game, quail is no longer available from the wild (the disappearance is blamed on over-enthusiastic netting on the islands of the Mediterranean during the birds' bi-annual migrations), and the small birds – thrushes, ortolans, fig-peckers – are no longer hunted, at least for commercial reasons. Nevertheless, French country-folk don't take kindly to being told what they can and cannot bring home for the pot and hunting is seen as a way of life, a right as well as a pleasure. Among isolated rural communities, it was a way of escaping routine domesticity in more ways than one. A friend and neighbour of mine in the Languedoc told me she always knew when her husband, under pretence of setting traps for rabbits, had visited his fancy woman across the valley because when he returned home, his clothes were perfumed with sarriette, a variety of thyme which only grew on the southern slopes of the hillside, along the path which led to her dwelling.

civet de lièvre

SLOW-COOKED HARE *in* RED WINE

A civet can be made with venison, rabbit, any game birds, or a mixture. Game is lean, dry meat which needs extra fat – petit salé (salt-cured belly pork or streaky bacon). To prepare your own petit salé, buy a thick slice of fatty belly pork, sprinkle with rough salt, cracked pepper and bay leaf, and leave overnight.

Serves 8–10

2 bay leaves
1 thyme sprig
1 rosemary sprig
1 teaspoon dried oregano
2 garlic cloves, roughly chopped
1 bottle robust red wine
1 tablespoon plain flour
½ teaspoon grated nutmeg
salt and freshly milled pepper
1 well–grown hare, trimmed and cut into small joints
4 tablespoons olive oil
500g (1lb 2oz) shallots or pickling onions, skinned
2–3 carrots, cut into chunks
1 thick slice petit salé (salt-cured belly pork), salted overnight, diced

TO FINISH
the hare's blood or 2 squares bitter black chocolate, chopped

1 Mix the bay leaves, thyme, rosemary, oregano, garlic and wine in a roomy bowl. Add the hare and turn pieces in the marinade. Cover and leave to absorb the flavours – overnight is best.

2 Mix the flour with the nutmeg and sat and pepper. Drain the joints, reserving the marinade, pat dry and dust with flour. Heat the oil in a large casserole and add the onions, carrots and petit salé (salt-cured belly pork). Fry until they caramelise a little and remove. Set aside on a plate.

3 Fry the pieces of hare until lightly browned. Add the reserved marinade and a cupful of water and bubble up. Replace the pork mixture. Turn down the heat, cover tightly and leave to simmer quietly for 1½–2 hours, until the meat is falling off the bone and the sauce is thick, rich and dark. Alternatively, the casserole can be transferred to the oven to cook very gently at 140°C (275°F, gas 1). Check occasionally and add a splash of boiling water if the casserole is drying out.

4 Stir in the blood or chocolate and cook gently for 1–2 minutes, stirring until the sauce has accepted the addition. Do not boil or the sauce will curdle. It's good today, better tomorrow.

lapin à la moutarde

RABBIT *with* MUSTARD

Although wild rabbit has a finer flavour, the hutch rabbits reared in every well-stocked French barnyard are well flavoured and guaranteed to be tender. When preparing rabbit for the pot, remember to remove the clear membrane that covers the saddle and hind legs or the meat will never be really tender however long you cook it. Use a sharp knife – you have to be brutal and waste a bit of flesh.

Serves 4

2 wild or 1 tame rabbit, cut into neat pieces
1 tablespoon plain flour, seasoned
4–5 tablespoons oil or melted butter
2 onions, finely chopped
1–2 thyme sprigs
1 glass white wine
600ml (1 pint) stock or water
salt and freshly milled pepper

TO FINISH
1 tablespoon mild Dijon mustard
1 tablespoon wholegrain mustard (Meaux)
4 tablespoons crème fraîche or double cream
buttered noodles or white rice to serve

1 Pick over the rabbit joints, removing any fluff or sharp splinters of bone. Toss the joints in the flour. Heat the oil or butter in a roomy pan and fry the joints until they sieze and brown a little. Remove and reserve.

2 Add the onions to the hot pan juices and fry gently until they soften and gild but do not let them brown further. Return the rabbit joints to the pan and add the thyme, wine and water or stock. Bubble up, scraping in any sticky bits from the pan, turn down the heat, season and cover loosely.

3 Leave to simmer gently for as long as it takes for the rabbit to be so tender it can be eaten with a fork. A young animal will be ready in 30–40 minutes, an older rabbit may take over 1 hour.

4 When the rabbit is perfectly tender, stir in the mustard and cream, bubble up again and serve with buttered noodles or plain white rice to soak up the juices.

pigeonneaux poêles aux bolets

GRILLED PIGEONS *with* MUSHROOMS

I n the days when self-sufficiency was possible, most rural households kept and fattened up a lot of pigeons for the pot. While the young birds (squabs) were tender enough for roasting, this recipe suited elderly birds that had outlived their usefulness as breeders, as well as wild birds of uncertain age that fed on the crops. The number of birds to cook depends on appetites. The recipe also works well with fillets from a saddle of hare, or magrets of wild duck (use a sharp knife to lift the breast fillets from the rib cage). A Gratin Dauphinoise (see page 92) is the perfect accompaniment.

Serves 4

4–8 pigeons
2 tablespoons olive oil
1 teaspoon dried thyme
salt and freshly milled pepper
1 onion, cut into chunks
1–2 carrots, cut into chunks
1 stick celery, chopped
1 small turnip, cut into chunks
a small bunch of parsley, thyme and bay leaf
a few peppercorns
50g (2oz) dried cep
150ml (¼ pint) madeira or dessert wine

TO FINISH
150g (3 oz) unsalted butter, cut into large dice and chilled
large bunch of watercress

1 Use a sharp knife to lift the pigeon breast fillets off their rib cages. Brush with oil, sprinkle with thyme and season with salt and freshly milled pepper. Wrap the breast fillets in cling film and reserve.

2 Roast the carcasses with a little of the oil and onion, carrots, celery and turnip for 15 minutes in a very hot oven. Transfer the roast mixture to a roomy saucepan. Add 900ml (1½ pints) water and drop in the herbs, a few peppercorns and a little salt. Bring to the boil, turn down the heat and cover loosely. Simmer gently for 1–2 hours.

3 Meanwhile, put the ceps in a cupful of hot water to soak and swell for 30 minutes. Strain, reserving the ceps, and add the soaking liquid to the pot.

4 Strain the stock, return it to the pot and add the soaked ceps. Bubble up, turn down the heat and simmer for about 30 minutes, until the liquid has reduced to 150ml (¼ pint) and the ceps are tender. Add the madeira or dessert wine and bubble up fiercely for a moment to evaporate the alcohol, then simmer until reduced to 4 tablespoons of well-flavoured sauce.

5 When you are nearly ready to serve, preheat the oven to 140°C (275°F, gas 1) and preheat the grill or heat a heavy frying pan. Make sure the fillets are at room temperature. Sear them in the pan or under the grill using very fierce heat for 60 seconds on each side. Then transfer to the oven and leave for a minimum of 10 minutes and maximum 25 minutes, for the meat to firm and settle, and lose its rawness. Pigeon breasts should be pink and juicy – if overcooked, they will be grey and tough.

6 Just before you are about to serve the pigeons, bring the sauce back to the boil and whisk in the nuggets of cold butter one by one until the sauce thickens and becomes shiny.

7 Slice the pigeon breasts diagonally into pretty pink slices. Transfer to warm plates, sauce generously and serve with a hank of watercress on the side.

Cookery is not chemistry. It is an art. It requires instinct and taste rather than exact measurements.

Marcel Boulestin

cailles aux raisins

ROAST QUAIL STUFFED *with* GRAPES

R emember Babette's Feast, when she tucked the little quails into the vol-au-vent cases? Small birds are always festive and farmed quail are deliciously tender – a real treat. Most people will manage two birds, some can eat three.

Serves 4

8–12 quail
¼ bottle white wine
2 tablespoons olive oil
1 teaspoon crumbled thyme
salt and freshly milled pepper
100g (4oz) small white grapes
100g (4oz) unsalted butter

TO FINISH
100g (4oz) small white grapes, skinned and seeds removed
large bunch of watercress

1 Marinate the birds for a few hours (or overnight in the fridge) in the white wine, olive oil, thyme, salt and pepper.

2 Preheat the oven to 200°C (400°F, gas 6). Remove the birds and pat them dry, reserving the marinade for the sauce. Tuck a whole grape or two and a knob of butter inside each quail. Mash the remaining butter with salt and pepper and rub it over the breasts. Place in a roasting tin.

3 Roast the birds for 20–30 minutes, until the little legs move easily in their joints. Remove the quail from the tin and reserve, covered loosely with foil, while you make the sauce.

4 Set the roasting tin on the heat and pour in the marinade. Bubble it up, scraping in all the sticky brown drippings. Cook until the alcohol has evaporated and the sauce looks glossy. Taste, season and stir in the grapes.

5 Serve the birds on a bed of watercress and hand the sauce separately.

meat

pot-au-feu

POT-SIMMERED BEEF

I learned how to prepare the classic Sunday boiled dinner
from my neighbours, subsistence farmers in the Languedoc,
when my children attended school in Castelnaudary. Beef was
considered a luxury since it had to be bought from the butcher.
The three different cuts of meat were so important that the dish
would not be made if one of them was lacking. The rib or skirt
is for flavour, the shin for strength and the knuckle or marrow
bone, or oxtail, for richness.

Serves 6–8

1kg (2¼lb) boneless rib of beef or skirt, tied with string
500g (1lb 2oz) shin of beef, tied with string
1 knuckle, marrow bone or oxtail, cut into chunks
3–4 large carrots, cut into chunks (save the trimmings)
2–3 large leeks, cut into chunks (save the trimmings)
2 onions, unskinned and quartered
½ teaspoon peppercorns
1–2 bay leaves
salt
1 head celery, preferably green, cut into chunks
2 small turnips, cut into chunks (save the trimmings)
500g (1lb 2oz) potatoes
½ small green cabbage, cut into wedges

1 Put the beef and bones in a large stew pan or earthenware casserole. Cover with 2 litres (3½ pints) cold water. Bring to the boil and skim off the foam.

2 Add the trimmings from the carrots and leeks, the onions, peppercorns, bay leaves and 1 teaspoon salt. Bring the water back to the boil, allow it to give one big belch and then turn down the heat. Simmer for 3 hours, by which time the meat should be tender.

3 Strain the broth, discarding the trimmings and the onion. Either return the meat to the broth and leave it to cool overnight, then lift off the solid layer of fat before you reheat the broth, or skim off the fat with a spoon while the broth is still hot, then return the meat to the broth.

4 Reheat the meat and broth and add the carrots, leeks, celery and turnips. Bring back to the boil, turn down the heat and simmer for 10 minutes. Add the potatoes, reheat to boiling, turn down the heat and simmer for another 10 minutes. Add the cabbage wedges and bring back to the boil. Simmer for 10 minutes more, until all the vegetables are tender.

5 Slice the meat into manageable pieces and arrange with the vegetables in a large warm serving dish. Serve moistened with a ladleful of stock, handing more separately as a sauce. Accompany with a bunch of small red radishes, rinsed but still with their leaves; salt-cured capers, well-rinsed and dressed with wine vinegar; and cornichons (very small pickled gherkins).

daube de bœuf

SLOW-COOKED BEEF *with* WINE AND OLIVES

*T*his is one of those slow-simmered winter stews, farmhouse fare, which takes its name from the pot in which it's cooked. The composition varies: this particular version comes from the olive-town of Nyons in Haute Provence. Dried orange zest adds a subtle hint of summer. To prepare your own, simply pare the zest from an orange, dry it on a window sill and store.

Serves 4–6

1kg (2¼lb) stewing beef, trimmed
250g (9oz) belly pork, diced
2 tablespoons pork lard or olive oil
1 onion, chopped
1 large carrot, diced
1 celery stick, diced
4 garlic cloves, crushed
500g (1lb 2oz) small shallots or pickling onions, peeled
2–3 tablespoons white brandy
1 tablespoon black olives (the wrinkly salted
little olives of Nyons are perfect)
1–2 curls dried orange zest
1 short cinnamon stick
1–2 bay leaves
250ml (8fl oz) strong red wine
salt and freshly milled pepper

1 Have ready a large round-bellied earthenware casserole or whichever pot you use to cook a stew. Cut the beef into bite-sized pieces. Remove the skin from the belly pork, then dice the meat and cut the skin into small squares.

2 Heat the lard or oil in a roomy frying pan and add the onion, carrot, celery and garlic. Fry them for a moment, then push them aside and add the shallots or baby onions. Fry gently until they take a little colour.

3 Push the vegetables aside, add the meat and let it brown a little. Sprinkle with the brandy and light it with a match to burn off the alcohol and caramelise the sugars in the meat.

4 Add the diced pork rind, carrot, olives, orange zest, cinnamon and bay leaf. The pork rind will melt into the broth and thicken the juices during the long cooking. Pour in the red wine and enough water to completely submerge the meat, season with pepper (no salt yet) and bubble up.

5 Turn down the heat and cover the pot tightly. (Seal it with a flour-and-water paste if the fit is not perfect.) Allow to simmer very gently over a low heat or transfer to the oven, set at 170°C (325°F, gas 3). Leave the daube to cook for 1½–2 hours, until the meat is so tender you can cut it with a spoon.

6 Remove the lid towards the end of the cooking to allow the juices to reduce and thicken. Taste and add salt before serving.

SERVING SUGGESTION ~ Serve with white rice or floury boiled potatoes dressed with chopped parsley. To follow, offer a winter salad of bitter leaves, such as dandelion, chicory and endive.

bœuf bourguignon

SLOW-COOKED BEEF *in* RED WINE

This is a dish of lean beef enriched with fat pork, cooked in the same type of wine you intend to drink with the dish – and that should be a robust red burgundy with plenty of tannin, nothing too light or sharp. Older recipes include a calf's foot, which is precooked and added along with the pork-skin. You can include a handful of button mushrooms if you wish – brown them in bacon fat at the same time as the onions.

Serves 6

1.5kg (3¼lb) rump or silverside, cut into bite-sized cubes
a small bunch of thyme, bay leaf and parsley
1 bottle burgundy or any robust red wine
1 tablespoon brandy
1 heaped tablespoon plain flour
½ teaspoon crushed allspice berries
salt and freshly milled pepper
250g (9oz) belly pork
1 tablespoon unsalted butter
600g (1lb) pickling onions, skinned
2 garlic cloves, crushed
250g (9oz) streaky bacon, finely diced

1 Put the beef in a roomy bowl with the herbs, wine and brandy. Leave to marinate overnight. Next day, remove the meat and shake it dry it over the bowl. Reserve the meat and the marinade.

2 Season the flour with allspice, salt and pepper. Pat the beef dry and dust lightly with the flour, then set aside. Skin the pork, roll up the skin and tie it in a roll. Cut the meat into cubes.

3 Heat a heavy flameproof casserole and gently fry the pork cubes in their own rich fat until they brown on all sides and produce plenty of oily drippings. Remove the meat and reserve.

4 Reheat the pan drippings if necessary (you may need a little butter) and fry the beef until it browns, then remove and

reserve. Reheat the pan drippings, add the onions, garlic and bacon and toss over the heat to brown everything a little.

5 Return the reserved meats to the pan, add the rolled-up pork skin and the marinade, bring to the boil and bubble up for 1–2 minutes until the liquor no longer smells of alcohol.

6 Turn down the heat, cover tightly and leave to simmer very gently for 2–3 hours. Alternatively, preheat the oven to 150°C (300°F, gas 2) and transfer the casserole to the oven. If you need to add liquid during cooking, make sure it is boiling.

7 When the meat is perfectly tender, remove the roll of pork-skin, cut it into fine strips and stir it back into the juices. Remove the herbs. Taste and adjust the seasoning. Serve the beef from its cooking pot.

SERVING SUGGESTION ~ Serve with plain buttered white rice or pommes de terre mousseline (see page 94) – mashed potato beaten with plenty of hot cream, butter and an egg yolk, and seasoned with nutmeg.

The discovery of a new dish does more for the happiness of mankind than the discovery of a new star.

Anthelme Brillat-Savarin

steak au poivre

PEPPERED STEAK

This is a simple dish, requiring nothing less than perfection in the raw materials. The tenderest steak, lightly marbled with golden fat; the most aromatic pepper; the freshest butter; and good wine. Curnonsky, styled the Prince of Gastronomes as much for his appetite as by virtue of authorship of the Larousse Gastronomique, gives two recipes for his favourite dish, one including shallots, the other omitting them. I have chosen the latter, as the man himself said, "Faites simple". Serve with crisp fat chips – frites – with a salad to follow.

Serves 4

4 steaks, about 350g (12oz) each
4 teaspoons cracked black peppercorns (use a mortar
and pestle to crack the pepper)
1 teaspoon salt
about 50g (2oz) unsalted butter
2 glasses white wine (half a glass per steak)

TO FINISH
chilled butter

1 Heat the serving plates. Coat each steak thoroughly in pepper, pressing the spice well in on both sides. Season each steak lightly with salt.

2 In a heavy pan, melt a nugget of butter per steak. When very hot, put in the steaks. Sear the meat on both sides, then continue cooking very slowly until they are cooked to your liking. Allow 2 minutes a side for very rare or up to 5 minutes for well done.

3 Remove the meat and transfer to the warm plates. Deglaze the pan by splashing in the wine and bubbling it up while scraping in all the little brown bits. Bubble to reduce by half. Whisk in an extra knob of butter to add gloss and thicken the sauce. Pour the sauce over the steaks.

entrecôte vigneronne

This rich Lyonnais version of the classic wine-sauced steak of the French bistro menu is deliciously simple. Choose well-hung steak with a generous lip of golden fat.

Serves 4

**4 thick-cut entrecôte steaks, about 250g (9oz) each
salt and coarsely milled pepper
75g (3oz) butter, chilled
2–3 shallots, finely chopped
1 onion, finely chopped
2–3 canned anchovy fillets, drained and finely chopped
120ml (4fl oz) robust red wine, preferably Burgundy**

1 Trim the steaks neatly, leaving plenty of creamy yellow fat, and season them on both sides. Melt 50g (2oz) of the butter in a heavy frying pan.

2 Place the steaks in the pan as soon as the butter begins to foam. Sear the meat on both sides, then turn down the heat a little and cook for 3 minutes on each side if you like your meat rare or 4 minutes for medium. "Well done" steak is unthinkable. Remove and reserve in a warm place for the meat to settle and firm up while you make the sauce.

3 Add the shallots, onion and anchovies to the juices in the pan, heat vigorously and cook for about 5 minutes, until the onions are lightly browned.

4 Stir in the wine, bring to boil and bubble fiercely for 1–2 minutes to evaporate the alcohol and concentrate the flavours. Cut the remaining cold butter into tiny pieces and stir them into the sauce to add gloss and finish. Reheat until the butter melts and forms an emulsion, and transfer to a warm sauceboat. Serve the sauce with the steaks.

SERVING SUGGESTION ~ Accompany the steaks with fine-cut chips – pommes allumettes – and hanks of watercress for the sake of the digestion.

entrecôte bordelaise

RIB STEAKS *with* BEEF MARROW AND RED WINE

*T*his is one of the great dishes of the world. The only
essential is a butcher who knows his business. The meat
should be of a satisfying carmine, marbled and edged with a
thick border of fat whose colour varies from buttery gold to
creamy white – the colour being dependant on breed, age and
diet – and the marrow-bones of impeccable freshness.

Serves 4

**4 entrecôte steaks, about 14oz (400g) each
oil or melted butter for brushing**

SAUCE
**1 tablespoon unsalted butter
2–3 shallots, finely chopped
4 tablespoons red wine (Bordeaux, naturally)
4 thick slices beef marrow (see opposite)
rough sea salt and freshly milled black pepper
freshly grated nutmeg
1 tablespoon chopped parsley**

TO SERVE
a big bunch of watercress

1 Have serving plates warming ready for the meat. Brush the steaks with oil or melted butter, and pepper lightly on both sides.

2 Preheat a ridged griddle pan. (If you have a charcoal barbecue, so much the better – use that.) Grill the steaks until done to your liking: allow 2 minutes a side for very rare or up to 5 minutes for well done. Transfer the steaks to hot plates and reserve in a warm place while you finish the sauce.

3 Heat the butter in a small pan and gently fry the shallot until it softens – do not let it brown. Add the red wine and bubble fiercely for 3–4 minutes until the smell of alcohol has disappeared. Slip in the slices of beef marrow and remove from the heat.

4 Spoon the marrow and sauce gently over the steaks – each should have its slice of marrow. Season with grainy sea salt, freshly milled pepper, a little nutmeg and a speckle of parsley. Serve immediately, with a generous hank of watercress on each plate.

PREPARING BEEF MARROW ~ Beef marrow or bone marrow – is found in marrow bones. Ask your butcher to saw a beef shin bone in short lengths. Take the package home, crack the bones with a hammer and lift out the soft yellow marrow inside. Poach the marrow for 1–2 minutes in simmering salted water – do not let the water boil. Lift the marrow out with care (it is fragile stuff), allow to cool, and slice it into thick medallions. You will probably have more than you need for the recipe – no matter – dice the rest and freeze it. You can use it to enrich sauces as if it were butter.

hachis parmentier

MEAT AND POTATO GRATIN

This sophisticated cottage pie was named for Monsieur Parmentier, the man responsible for persuading the French to plant potatoes.

∽◦∽

Serves 4

50g (2oz) butter
500g (1lb 2oz) minced lamb or leftover cooked lamb,
finely chopped
1 garlic clove, chopped
1 large onion, finely chopped
100g (4oz) mushrooms, chopped
½ teaspoon dried thyme
1 tablespoon chopped parsley
1 heaped tablespoon plain flour
½ teaspoon ground allspice
1–2 bay leaves
250ml (8fl oz) stock or a mixture of white wine and water
salt and freshly milled pepper

TOPPING
1.5kg (2½lb) potatoes boiled and mashed with butter,
milk, salt, pepper, a little nutmeg
1 egg yolk, forked up
1 tablespoon grated cheese
1 large nugget unsalted butter

1 Melt the butter in a heavy saucepan and fry the meat, garlic and onion until the meat changes colour. If using cooked lamb, add it after the onion and garlic have cooked a little and just let it feel the heat. Stir from time to time to prevent sticking. Remove and reserve.

2 Reheat the pan drippings, add the mushrooms, salt lightly, sprinkle with thyme and parsley, and fry until they yield their juices, dry and begin to sizzle and brown. Remove and reserve.

3 Return the meat and onion mixture to the pan, sprinkle in the flour and fry for a moment. Season with allspice and pepper, add the bay leaves and stock or water and wine, and bubble up. Turn down the heat and leave to simmer for 20–30 minutes, until the meat is tender.

4 Meanwhile, preheat the oven to 200°C (400°F, gas 6). Taste the meat and adjust the seasoning. The mixture may need a little more water – it should be juicy rather than dry.

5 Butter a gratin dish and spread a layer of mashed potato (about a third) in the base. Cover with the meat, then with half the remaining potato. Spread with the reserved mushrooms. Cover with a final topping of potato.

6 Fork up the potato and glaze it with egg yolk. Sprinkle with grated cheese and dot with butter. Finish in the oven for 20–30 minutes to reheat the layers and brown and crisp the top.

navarin d'agneau

SLOW-COOKED LAMB *with* BABY VEGETABLES

T ender lamb and young vegetables, in season at the same time, are combined in this classic stew from the bourgeois tradition. Ask the butcher for some lamb bones for a stock.

Serves 4–6

2 tablespoons oil or melted unsalted butter
1kg (2¼lb) boneless lamb, such as neck fillet, shoulder
or breast, trimmed and diced
1 tablespoon diced lean Bayonne ham or bacon
20 small shallots or baby onions
1–2 carrots, diced
salt and freshly milled pepper
1 tablespoon plain flour
2 garlic cloves
1 tablespoon tomato puree
a small bunch of parsley, thyme and a bay leaf
1 litre (1¾ pints) lamb or vegetable stock

TO FINISH
new potatoes, fresh peas, young beans,
baby carrots, baby turnips
2 tablespoons chopped parsley

1 Heat the oil or butter in a straight-sided sauté pan or heavy frying pan. Add the lamb, ham or bacon, shallots or onions and carrots. Fry over a very brisk heat, stirring to brown the ingredients on all sides. Season with salt and pepper.

2 Spoon out any visible fat from the pan, sprinkle with the flour and toss over the heat for a couple of minutes to allow the flour to brown a little.

3 Add the garlic, tomato puree, herbs and stock. Bring to the boil, bubble up for a minute or two, turn down the heat and simmer for 40–60 minutes, until the lamb is perfectly tender and the juices are concentrated and rich. Alternatively transfer the ingredients to an ovenproof casserole and cook in the oven for 1 hour at 160°C (325°F, gas 3).

4 For a classic presentation, cook the baby vegetables separately in a ladleful of the stock from the lamb. Taste the lamb and adjust the seasoning. Pile the lamb in a warm serving dish and sprinkle with chopped parsley. Arrange the vegetables over the navarin before serving.

épaule d'agneau en pistache

POT-ROAST LAMB *with* LOTS OF GARLIC

For this recipe, a boned-out shoulder of lamb (it could be a leg or a saddle) is cooked with an unreasonable amount of garlic, the diagnostic ingredient of a pistache. Choose the mild rosy-skinned garlic of Provence and be brave – the quantity may seem like a lot, but the long, slow cooking melts the flesh, thickens the juices and gentles the flavour. Partridge, pheasant and pigeons all benefit from the same treatment. Potatoes sautéed with rosemary are the perfect accompaniment.

Serves 4–6

1 shoulder of lamb, boned, rolled and tied
salt and freshly milled pepper
2 tablespoons fresh pork lard or goose fat
1 thick slice, about 100g (4oz) unsmoked raw ham or lean
unsmoked bacon, cut into small cubes
50 garlic cloves, about 5 whole heads, skinned but left whole
150ml (¼ pint) white wine
(not too dry – a sweetish wine complements the garlic)
150ml (¼ pint) lamb or vegetable stock
a small bunch of thyme, rosemary, bay leaf, parsley
a small piece of dried orange peel

1 Preheat the oven to 180°C (350°F, gas 4). Wipe the meat and rub it with very little salt and plenty of pepper.

2 Heat a roomy casserole which will just accommodate the meat and garlic. Melt the lard or goose fat in the casserole, add the ham and the garlic, and fry them until the garlic softens. Remove and reserve.

3 Turn the lamb in the hot drippings to brown it a little on all sides. Add the reserved ham and garlic, wine and stock – the liquid should come about half way up the meat. Tuck in the herbs and orange peel and bring to the boil. Cover tightly and transfer to the oven.

4 Leave to cook for 1 hour, until the meat is perfectly tender and the garlic cloves melted and soft. Transfer the lamb to a warm serving dish, tent with foil, shiny side in, and leave to rest for 10 minutes before slicing into neat rounds.

5 Meanwhile, remove the herbs and peel from the cooking liquor. Mash the garlic into the cooking juices to give the sauce body and fragrance, and spoon it over the meat.

blanquette de veau

POACHED VEAL *in* CREAM SAUCE

A delicate dish that needs little preparation but requires a great deal of patience: it is very soothing both to make and to eat. Good for invalids, children and toothless old granddads.

Serves 6–8

2kg (4½lb) boneless veal shoulder, trimmed and cut into cubes
2 litres (3½ pints) veal or chicken stock, plus a little extra
1 small onion stuck with 2–3 cloves
2 carrots, diced
1 leek, finely chopped
a small bunch of parsley, thyme and a bay leaf
½ teaspoon white peppercorns
75g (3oz) unsalted butter
75g (3oz) plain flour
250g (9oz) button mushrooms
juice of 1 lemon
3 egg yolks
150ml (¼ pint) double cream
¼ teaspoon freshly grated nutmeg
sea salt and freshly milled pepper

TO FINISH
finely chopped parsley

1 Put the veal in a roomy cooking pot with the main quantity of stock. Bring to the boil and skim carefully, removing all the grey foam that rises.

2 Add the onion, carrots, leek, herbs, peppercorns and salt. Bring back to the boil, turn down the heat and cover loosely. Leave to simmer gently (no bubbles should break the surface) for about 1½ hours, until the veal is perfectly tender and the broth strong and clear. Skim the broth every now and again, and add boiling water, if necessary, to maintain the volume of liquid.

3 Remove and discard the herbs, onion and carrots with a draining spoon and discard. Remove and reserve the meat. Strain the broth carefully, pouring it through a sieve lined with a clean cloth. Return the broth to the pot – you need the full 2 litres (3½ pints).

4 Turn your attention to the sauce. Mash the butter with the flour until it makes a smooth paste – this is a beurre manie. Whisk the paste into the broth and reheat, whisking throughout, until boiling. Reduce the heat and simmer for 30 minutes or so, until the sauce has reduced by a third of its volume and is smooth and shiny.

5 Meanwhile, bring a little veal or chicken stock to the boil. Add the mushrooms and 1 teaspoon of the lemon juice and cook for 5 minutes. Add the reserved meat and reheat gently, then transfer to a warmed serving dish.

6 Fork the remaining lemon juice with the egg yolks. Remove the sauce from the heat and whisk in the cream, then the egg

yolk mixture. Season with a little nutmeg. Return the pan to the heat and simmer for a few minutes, stirring with a wooden spoon, until all is smooth. Do not let the sauce boil. Taste and season with salt and pepper.

7 Pour the sauce over the meat and shower with the parsley.

choucroute

SAUERKRAUT *with* SAUSAGES

This stupendous pork-and-cabbage one-pot dish is prepared in Alsace and where the German influence is strong. It takes its name from the diagnostic ingredient, salt-barelled cabbage, choucroute or sauerkraut.

Serves 8

**2kg (4½lb) sauerkraut
4 thin slices fresh pork fat
1 large carrot, sliced
1 onion stuck with 2–3 cloves
a small bunch of parsley, a bay leaf and thyme
1 teaspoon juniper berries, crushed
1 pork knuckle
500g (1lb 2oz) smoked pork loin or bacon in one piece
8 thick slices ham
1 large garlic sausage, about 1kg (2¼lb), pricked
8 tablespoons goose fat or freshly prepared pork lard
2 glasses white wine
about 900ml (1½ pints) stock or water
8 large frankfurters
salt and pepper**

TO SERVE
boiled potatoes/pickled cucumbers/mild mustard

1   Put the sauerkraut in a bowl of cold water and work it with
    your fingers to loosen the strands. Drain off the water. Repeat
twice, squeezing to remove as much of the liquid as possible.
Spread the drained sauerkraut on a clean tea towel and leave to
dry for 1–2 hours. Season with pepper – it should not need salt.

2   Preheat the oven to 160°C (325°F, gas 3). Line a roomy
    flameproof and ovenproof braising pot or casserole with
the pork fat. Spread half the sauerkraut on the fat, then add the
carrot, onion, herbs, juniper berries, pork knuckle, smoked pork
or bacon, ham and garlic sausage in layers. Sprinkle with half the
goose fat or lard and top with the remaining sauerkraut.

3   Pour in the white wine and enough stock or water to ensure
    that all the ingredients are moistened. Finish with the
remaining goose fat. Bring the ingredients to the boil, cover
tightly with a lid or foil and transfer to the oven.

4   Leave to cook gently for 2 hours, until almost all the liquid
    has been absorbed. After 30–40 minutes, remove the garlic
sausage and keep it warm. After 1 hour, remove and reserve the
bacon. After 1½ hours, remove and reserve the smoked pork.

5   To finish, 20 minutes before the end of cooking, heat the
    frankfurters in enough simmering water to cover – do not
allow the water to boil.

6   Pile the sauerkraut on a heated serving dish – a long and
    narrow dish is traditional. Remove and discard the onion and
separate the meats. Pile the meats, sliced as appropriate, on top
of the sauerkraut: the traditional arrangement is a lower layer of
sliced ham topped with alternating overlapping slices of bacon,

sausage and pork. Finally, the frankfurters should be arranged around the edge.

7 Serve very hot, on hot plates, with a big bowl of plain cooked potatoes, pickled cucumbers and mild mustard.

CHOUCROUTE ~ The choucroute is prepared with finely shredded white cabbage, which undergoes a process of light fermentation. This miraculous transformation not only makes it taste good but preserves the vitamin content and makes it easier to digest. The brine is used as a cure for everything from hangovers and morning sickness to the aftermath of childbirth.

The new-season choucroute is traditionally eaten with fresh pork and sausage after the autumn pig-killing, which conveniently coincides with the wine harvest. It is then eaten with salt pork and smoked sausages throughout winter, and reappears with goose for the Christmas festivities. It takes a bow on New Year's Day, as an oblation for the year's renewal, and the last of the barrel is scraped in Lent, to be eaten with fresh fish as soon as the spring thaw releases the fishing boats from harbour.

SWEETBREADS (RIS) ~ To prepare, put the sweetbreads in a bowl and cover them with salted water. Leave for 24 hours to soak out any traces of blood. Clean and wipe. Then put them into boiling water with a few peppercorns and 1 tablespoon vinegar. Bring back to the boil and simmer for 15 minutes. Drain and remove all traces of skin and sinew. Press between two plates, placing a weight on top, until cold and firm. Cut into squares. They are now ready to be finished – stewed in butter; sauced with mushrooms and cream; egged-and-breadcrumbed and fried – the choice is yours.

BRAINS (CERVELLES) ~ Soak them first in salted water (2–4 hours depending on the size of the brain). Remove the covering membrane and wipe the meats carefully. Soak them for a further 1 hour to get rid of any remaining blood. Simmer as for sweetbreads – brains will need an extra 10 minutes' cooking. Store them in their cooking liquid if they are not be used at once.

TRIPE (TRIPES) ~ This is neither more nor less than the lining of the stomach of a ruminant, preferably a beef animal. But be warned, French butchers don't necessarily steam and bleach their tripe before they sell it to you, so it may be spongy and somewhat unappetising until well-scrubbed and scalded. All ruminants, including the cow, have 4 stomachs – 3 are labelled gras double, the fourth is just tripe. All four are used for France's most famous tripe-dish, tripes a la mode de Caen. To prepare the recipe for six, buy 2 kg (4lb) ready-scrubbed tripe and stew very gently – preferably in a round-

226

bellied, narrow-mouthed tripière – with a couple of blanched, split pig's trotters, a handful of sliced carrots, a couple of thickly sliced onions, parsley, bay leaf, a splash of calvados, peppercorns, salt and enough cider to cover. When the tripe is perfectly tender – 3–4 hours at a very gentle simmer – serve with boiled potatoes and eat with a spoon.

LIVER (FOIE) ~ Calves' liver is, quite rightly, considered the most delicate of variety meats, and foie de veau à l'anglaise – calves' liver English-style – is the most appreciated. To prepare for four servings of à l'anglaise, have your butcher slice 750g (1lb) calves' liver in finger-length fillets, soak in milk for half an hour, drain, toss in a little seasoned flour and fry in butter over a high heat with a handful of diced bacon – the liver should still be pink and juicy.

KIDNEYS (ROGNONS) ~ Veal kidneys are the most prized of the group: to prepare kidneys à la bordelaise for two, slice a veal kidney thickly (nick out the fatty white core), soak in water with a splash of wine vinegar for 10 minutes, drain, toss in a little seasoned flour, fry in butter for a minute or two till the meat stiffens, add a splash of madeira and a glass of red Bordeaux, bubble up to evaporate the alcohol and thicken the sauce, and finish with a spoonful of mild Bordeaux mustard. Rognons blancs – white kidneys – the tactful way of describing testicles, animelles – can be prepared in the same way.

ris de veau à la crème

VEAL SWEETBREADS *with* CREAM

Two varieties of sweetbreads are sold under the same
name: the pancreas (elongated in shape and found near
the stomach) and the thymus glands (rounded and to be found
at the base of the throat).

Serves 4

4 veal sweetbreads
a few black peppercorns
1 tablespoon white wine vinegar

SAUCE
2 tablespoons unsalted butter
2 tablespoons finely chopped button mushrooms
1 tablespoon plain flour
150ml (¼ pint) white wine
150ml (¼ pint) double cream
1 egg yolk, forked to blend
salt and freshly milled pepper
rounds of bread, fried in butter, to serve

1 To prepare the sweetbreads, put them in a bowl and cover with cold water, then add a little salt. Set in a cool place for 24 hours to soak out any traces of blood. Clean and wipe.

2 Poach the drained sweetbreads for 3 minutes in boiling water with the peppercorns and vinegar. Drain and remove all traces of skin and sinew. Press between two weighted plates until cold and firm – at least 1 hour. Slice thickly.

3 Meanwhile make the sauce. Melt the butter in a small saucepan and fry the mushrooms gently for 2–3 minutes. Sprinkle with the flour, stir over the heat until the butter has been absorbed, then add the wine. Bubble up, whisking over the heat, until the sauce no longer smells of raw alcohol.

4 Stir in the cream and the egg yolk, reheat until just below boiling, then slip in the sweetbreads. Reheat gently, taste and season with salt and pepper, and serve on little rounds of bread fried in butter.

pieds de porc sainte-ménéhould

BREADED PIG'S TROTTERS

*T*he chief pleasure of a trotter is texture – long, slow
cooking makes the meat and skin soft and gelatinous.
*The secret is the slow stewing in a wine-flavoured court
bouillon, cooking broth. If you start them first thing in the
morning you can leave them to simmer all day.*

Serves 4–8

**4 pig's trotters, singed, scalded and scraped
1 onion, cut into chunks
1 carrot, cut into chunks
1 celery stick, cut into chunks
1 bay leaf
a few peppercorns
1 glass dry white wine**

TO FINISH
**4 tablespoons fresh breadcrumbs
1 garlic clove, finely chopped
2 tablespoons chopped parsley
125g (4½oz) unsalted butter, melted
salt and freshly milled pepper**

1 Split the trotters in half lengthwise, tie the halves back together again in pairs and pack them in a flameproof casserole that can also be put in the oven. Add the onion, carrot, celery, bay leaf and peppercorns. Add the wine and enough water to cover the ingredients completely.

2 Bring to the boil, cover loosely and cook steadily for 30 minutes. Top up with boiling water, turn down the heat and cover tightly, sealing with a flour-and-water paste if the lid does not fit perfectly. Preheat the oven to 140°C (275°F, gas 1).

3 Place in the oven and leave to simmer very gently for at least 8 hours, until the trotters are really soft. Leave them to cool in their liquid.

4 Drain the trotters and reserve a ladleful of the cooking liquid. Untie and arrange in a gratin dish, cut side up. Remove the hard central bones. Preheat the grill.

5 To finish, mix the breadcrumbs, garlic and parsley. Top the trotters with the breadcrumb mixture, season with salt and pepper and trickle with melted butter. Grill to gild and crisp the topping.

cervelles au beurre noir

BRAINS *with* BLACK BUTTER

A delicate dish. French gourmets have a more robust view of what is good to eat and they would not dream of discarding the best bits of any beast.

Serves 4

1 calf's brain or 3 lambs' brains
½ teaspoon peppercorns
1 bay leaf
1 tablespoon vinegar
salt and freshly milled pepper

TO FINISH
125g (4½oz) unsalted butter
a little plain flour
1 tablespoon vinegar
1 tablespoon drained capers

1 Soak the brains in salted water for 2–4 hours, depending on size. Drain, pat dry, remove the covering membrane and wipe carefully. Soak for another hour in fresh salted water to get rid of any remaining blood.

2 Bring a small pan of water seasoned with salt, the peppercorns, bay leaf and vinegar to the boil and slip in the brains. Bring back to the boil, turn down the heat and simmer for 10–15 minutes, depending on size. Drain well and press between two plates until cold and firm.

3 Meanwhile, begin by clarifying the butter ready for finishing the dish: melt it in a small pan. As soon as it oils, pour the clear liquid off the top and reserve, discarding the milky liquid that has drifted to the bottom.

4 Slice the brains into bite-sized squares, dust thoroughly with a little seasoned flour, and fry in a tablespoon of the clarified butter until browned. Remove the brains and reserve.

5 Heat the remaining butter in the pan. As soon as it turns a nutty brown – do not let it burn – add the vinegar and the capers, reheat and spoon the butter over the brains.

sauces

sauce béchamel

BASIC WHITE SAUCE

Béchamel is one of three foundation sauces on which a wide range of others are based; sauce espagnole and sauce velouté are the other two. A béchamel rarely stands on its own but serves as a vehicle for other ingredients – cooked, finely diced or chopped chicken, meat, fish or vegetables (particularly spinach). These can then be transformed into plats composées, combined dishes. They can be spread in a gratin dish, finished with a topping of grated cheese or breadcrumbs and butter, and browned under the grill until it is bubbling and gilds.

Makes 600ml (1 pint) coating sauce

50g (2oz) unsalted butter
50g (2oz) plain flour
600ml (1 pint) full-cream milk
salt and freshly milled pepper
¼ teaspoon freshly grated nutmeg (optional)

1 Melt the butter in a heavy-based saucepan. Stir in the flour and let it fry for a moment until it looks sandy – do not let it take colour. This is a white roux.

2 Allow the pan to cool while you heat the milk in another pan. Remove the milk from the heat just before it boils.

3 Whisk the boiling milk slowly into the roux, return the pan to a gentle heat and stir with a wooden spoon until the sauce is smooth, no longer tastes of raw flour, and coats the back of the spoon.

4 Taste and season with salt, pepper and a pinch of grated nutmeg (if using). To keep the sauce for later, drop a few pieces of cold butter over the surface to melt and prevent a skin from forming.

SAUCES DERIVED FROM SAUCE BÉCHAMEL ~ For a richer sauce, use single cream instead of milk.

Sauce mornay ~ Add 3–4 tablespoons grated cheese and reheat gently until the cheese melts.
● For seafood gratins, fold cooked seafood (fillets of sole, turbot or salmon; peeled prawns; dressed crab; scallops; or mussels) into sauce mornay and spread in a gratin dish. Finish with more grated cheese or breadcrumbs and slip under the grill to brown.
● For individual fish gratins, use well-scrubbed scallop shells as the containers.
● The milk can be replaced with the same volume of white wine and fish stock and finished with an extra knob of butter or 1 tablespoon cream.

Sauce soubise ~ This is an onion sauce based on béchamel. Cook 400g (14oz) finely chopped onion in 50g (2oz) butter until tender (do not let the onion brown). Puree with a spoonful of cream. Stir the puree into the béchamel, reheat, taste and season.
● A soubise is traditionally served as a sauce for hard-boiled eggs or plain boiled potatoes.

Sauce duxelles ~ Make a basic béchamel with white wine, chicken stock and cream instead of milk. Gently cook 300g (11oz) chopped mushrooms (wild or cultivated) in about 50g (2oz) unsalted butter – keep going until the juices have all evaporated but do not let the fungi brown. Stir the cooked mushrooms into the sauce.

- Good for filling vols-au-vent or choux buns.
- Perfect as a coating sauce for the meat from a boiled chicken – spread in a gratin dish, coat with the sauce, sprinkle with fresh breadcrumbs, dot with butter and gild under the grill.

Sauce panada ~ This is a thick white sauce base which serves as a vehicle for other ingredients. Halve or quarter the volume of liquid to fat and flour, depending on the density of the sauce required for the recipe. Experience will tell you what you need.
- A panada can be diluted with other liquids – broth or wine – to make a pouring sauce, or used as the basis for a savoury soufflé – suitably flavoured with grated cheese, diced ham, finely chopped shrimp or chopped cooked spinach.
- As the basis for croquettes, make a panada following the béchamel recipe, but with 300ml (½ pint) milk or stock. Combine with chopped leftover cooked chicken or meat; cooked mushrooms; or grated cheese. Leave to cool and firm up overnight in the fridge. Then form it into little bolsters, dust in seasoned flour, dip in forked-up egg and coat with a jacket of breadcrumbs. Allow the coating to set for 1–2 hours before deep-frying the croquettes. The temperature of the oil should be sufficiently high to crisp the coating while allowing the interior to heat – if it is too hot, the jacket will burn; too cool and it will burst. Practice makes perfect.

sauce espagnole

BASIC BROWN SAUCE

O ne of the three most important sauces of the French kitchen (the other two are the white béchamel and sauce velouté), this dark, rich meat-based sauce takes its identity and character from the salt-cured wind-dried ham of Bayonne. Bayonne ham is closely identified with the serrano hams which colour and flavour every Spanish stew – hence the name Spanish sauce. The French refinement is the inclusion of jambon de Bayonne in the mirepoix, a flavouring-mix that adds depth and complexity to the finished sauce. While sauce espagnole needs no further attention as an enhancement for meat-based dishes, it also provides the foundation for other sauces.

Makes about 600ml (1 pint)

25g (1oz) unsalted butter
1 tablespoon finely diced Bayonne ham
1 large carrot, diced
1 onion or 2 shallots, finely chopped
1 celery stick, finely chopped
2 tablespoons chopped mushrooms
1 bay leaf
1 small thyme sprig
25g (1oz) plain flour
1 litre (1¾ pints) strong meat stock, heated
600ml (1 pint) chopped tomatoes
salt and freshly milled pepper

1 Melt half the butter in a heavy, preferably copper-based, pan. Add the ham, carrot, onion or shallots, celery, mushrooms, bay leaf and thyme, and fry very gently for 20–30 minutes until soft and lightly caramelised. Remove and reserve – this is a basic mirepoix, the classic flavouring-fry of the French kitchen.

2 Melt the rest of the butter in the pan, sprinkle in the flour and stir over the heat until the mixture turns a deep biscuit colour – mahogany is too dark – and remove immediately. Add a splash of stock to halt the cooking process.

3 Return the mixture to the heat and bubble up, whisking until you have a smooth sauce base – a caramel-coloured panada. Whisk in the remaining stock and bring back to the boil.

4 Add the reserved mirepoix and the tomatoes and bubble up again, beating to amalgamate everything thoroughly. Turn down the heat and leave to simmer very gently – no bubbles should break the surface – for 2–3 hours, until the sauce has reduced by half and it is well-flavoured and a little sticky. Skim the sauce every now and then during cooking.

5 Allow to cool a little, then pass the sauce through a fine sieve or, even better, strain it through a muslin cloth. To prevent a skin from forming, drop a few scraps of butter over the surface to melt. Use as the foundation for other sauces to accompany plain-grilled or spit-roasted meats.

SAUCES DERIVED FROM SAUCE ESPAGNOLE ～

Sauce Robert ～ Make 600ml (1 pint) sauce espagnole and add 150ml (¼ pint) white wine and 4 tablespoons white wine vinegar. Bubble up until reduced by a third. Remove from the heat and stir in 1 tablespoon Dijon mustard.
• Use to sauce grilled pork chops, pan-grilled magrets de canard (duck breasts – start cooking them skin side down and leave them pink), spit-roast rabbit or poached eggs.

Sauce bordelaise ～ Make 600ml (1 pint) sauce espagnole and add 300ml (½ pint) light red wine (a Bordeaux, for authenticity) and bubble up until reduced by a third. Poach 125g (4oz) beef-marrow in salted water for 10 minutes. Drain carefully, cut off and reserve 4–6 slices, and dice the rest. Reheat the sauce gently and stir in 1 tablespoon unsalted butter (cut into small pieces), the cubed marrow and 1 tablespoon finely chopped parsley.

- Use to sauce grilled entrecôte steaks, topping each steak with one of the reserved marrow slices.
- Use the sauce as a binding agent for diced cooked beef or lamb for a gratin. Spread in a gratin dish, top with breadcrumbs and finely chopped parsley and dot with butter. Slip the gratin under the grill to crisp and bubble.

Sauce madère ~ Make 600ml (1 pint) sauce espagnole and add 150ml (¼ pint) Madeira, then bubble up until reduced by a quarter.

- Use to sauce hot ham slices or pan-grilled pork escalopes.
- Use as the binding agent for diced cooked meat – lamb, pork or beef – when making a gratin, as for sauce bordelaise.

Sauce périgourdine ~ Make 600ml (1 pint) sauce madère, stir in 1 tablespoon diced black truffle and reheat gently. For extra richness, melt in a spoonful of mashed pâté de foie gras or Confit de Foie Gras (see page 28).

- Use to sauce grilled magret de canard (duck breast), breast of chicken or guinea fowl.
- Use as the binding agent for cooked poultry or game when making a gratin as for sauce bordelaise.

Sauce au poivre ~ Make 600ml (1 pint) sauce espagnole and stir in 1 teaspoon well-crushed peppercorns (do this in a mortar). Bring to the boil and simmer for 10–15 minutes, until the sauce is thoroughly impregnated with the pepper. Stir in 2–3 tablespoons double cream, bubble up again and use to sauce grilled steaks.

sauce velouté

VELOUTÉ SAUCE

The third member of the roux-based group of French sauces – the other two are espagnole and béchamel. This smooth golden sauce is made by simmering a well-reduced flour-thickened chicken or veal stock (or a fish fumet, if you intend the sauce for a fish dish). For a paler result, instead of cooking a roux, thicken the sauce with a beurre manie – flour worked to a paste with its own volume of cold butter. This sauce can be used as the basis for a chicken, vegetable or fish gratin.

Makes about 1 litre (1¾ pints)

75g (3oz) unsalted butter or goose fat
75g (3oz) plain flour
1.5 litres (2¾ pints) strong chicken or veal stock
small knob of butter to finish (optional)

1 In a roomy, heavy-bottomed pan, melt the butter or goose fat. Sprinkle in the flour and stir until it looks sandy.

2 Pour in the stock, whisking to prevent lumps from forming, and bring to the boil. Allow the sauce to give one big belch, turn down the heat and simmer gently, stirring regularly, for 30 minutes or so, until the sauce has lost a third of its volume and is smooth and shiny. If preparing the sauce in advance, float a few scraps of butter over the surface to prevent a skin from forming.

SAUCES DERIVED FROM THE VELOUTÉ ~

Sauce allemande ~ Prepare a chicken velouté and cook it for an extra 30 minutes. Prepare the same volume of stock as sauce, flavouring it with mushroom peelings, strain it and add to the sauce. Simmer gently for another 30 minutes until the sauce forms a thick coating on the back of a wooden spoon. Remove from the heat and allow to cool a little. Fork 2 egg yolks with 1 tablespoon double cream and whisk into the sauce. Reheat the sauce gently, whisking until well-blended, and remove from the heat before it boils. Season with a little freshly grated nutmeg.
• Use to sauce sautéed liver or kidneys; poached, sliced sweetbreads or brains; or poached eggs. To sauce fish, apply the same method using a fish velouté.

Sauce poulette ~ Finish a sauce allemande (as above) with the juice of 1 lemon and 2 tablespoons finely chopped parsley.
• Serve with poached chicken or use as a sauce for vineyard snails (see page 30).

Sauce suprême ~ Finish a sauce allemande with 2–3 tablespoons double cream and a squeeze of lemon juice.
● Use to sauce poached or plain-roast barnyard birds – chicken, guinea fowl or duck.

Sauce aux câpres ~ To a chicken or fish velouté, add 1 tablespoon well-drained pickled capers.
● Use to sauce boiled beef from Pot-au-feu (see page 200) or serve with poached fish, such as turbot, cod or salmon.

Sauce Nantua ~ Prepare a fish velouté and simmer to reduce by half. Add an equal volume each of single cream and fish stock made with crustacean debris – heads and shells of crayfish, prawn, lobster and/or shrimp. Bubble up, reduce the heat and leave to simmer gently for 30–40 minutes, until reduced by a third. Season the sauce with a little cayenne pepper and whisk in a few nuggets of chilled, unsalted butter.
● Serve with poached fillets of sole or as a sauce for lobster, prawns or scallops.

beurre blanc

MELTED BUTTER SAUCE

This simple emulsion of melted butter and wine vinegar is delicate and delicious. Make more than you think you need – people can never get enough of it.

Serves 4

**2 shallots or 1 small onion, finely chopped
6 tablespoons white wine vinegar
250g (9oz) unsalted butter, chilled and
chopped into small pieces**

1 Cook the shallots or onion with the vinegar in a small pan. When the vinegar has reduced by half, to about 4 tablespoons, strain it and discard the shallots or onion.

2 Return the vinegar to the pan. Whisk in the butter, gradually adding it in small pieces, with the pan over a very low heat or by the side of the heat so that the butter melts into a thick sauce. Do not let the sauce boil. If, in spite of your best efforts, the mixture splits, let the sauce cool. Pour it out of the pan and start again with a tablespoon of boiling water, gradually whisking in the split sauce.

sauce hollandaise

HOLLANDAISE SAUCE

This hot butter sauce thickened with egg yolks is made in much the same way as a béarnaise (see page 250), though the flavouring is lemon juice rather than a reduction of vinegar and shallot. This is a delicate sauce well suited to the white-fleshed fish, such as sole, turbot, plaice, cod, haddock or scallops, that are caught in the cold waters of the North Atlantic. It also goes well with soft-coddled or poached eggs and is perfect with spring vegetables, particularly new potatoes, cauliflower and asparagus. This method is a little unusual but it works.

Makes about 600ml (1 pint)

500g (1lb 2oz) unsalted butter
5 egg yolks
2 tablespoons lemon juice
salt

1 First clarify the butter: melt it gently in a small pan until runny. Continue heating gently until the fat and the whey separate, allowing the water to sink to the bottom. You can now pour the liquid butter from the surface leaving the whey behind, or allow the mixure to cool and lift off the solids, discarding the liquid beneath.

2 Put 4 tablespoons boiling water and the clarified butter in a fairly small saucepan of either enamel or copper lined with tin but not aluminium (which reacts with the acidity in the lemon, turning the sauce green). Place the pan into a second saucepan half filled with cold water. Alternatively, use a double-boiler.

3 Place the pans over a moderate heat. Fork the egg yolks with 2 tablespoons cold water and whisk them into the butter. Stir with a wooden spoon until the mixture thickens to the consistency of a pouring custard. When the water in the outer saucepan boils, the sauce will be thickened enough.

4 Remove from the heat and add the lemon juice slowly – if you add it too fast, the sauce will split and you will have to emulsify it again with a quick blitz in a blender. Taste and add salt.

sauce béarnaise

BÉARNAISE SAUCE

This sauce of butter and egg yolk is flavoured with a robust reduction of wine vinegar, shallot and tarragon and served with grilled meat. It is a speciality of Béarn, birthplace of Henri 1V, royal gourmet and a man much admired for his desire to put a chicken in every Frenchman's pot. The cooking of Béarn is rich and luxurious, making plentiful use of goose fat in everyday cooking, saving the butter for best. Serve with grilled meat (steaks, lamb chops, veal cutlets, pork escalopes), or grilled fish (swordfish, tuna, mackerel – nothing too delicate).

Makes about 300ml (½ pint)

5 tablespoons wine vinegar
1 shallot, finely chopped
2–3 tarragon and chervil sprigs
4 large egg yolks
250g (9oz) unsalted butter, chilled and diced
1 tablespoon tarragon leaves
salt and white pepper

1 Put the vinegar, shallots, tarragon and chervil in a small enamel pan, bring to the boil and bubble fiercely until the volume is reduced by half. Remove the pan from the heat, strain and allow the liquid to cool a little.

2 Meanwhile, whisk the egg yolks with 2 tablespoons cold water in a bowl. Whisk in the vinegar reduction. Place the bowl over a pan of simmering water. Whisk the sauce over a gentle heat until the mixture thickens like a custard.

3 Add the cold butter piece by piece, whisking throughout, until you have a thickish, spoonable sauce. If the mixture looks like curdling – separating or scrambling – remove the pan from the heat and place the base in cold water, then whisk in a little cold water and carry on whisking until the sauce regains its smoothness. Stir in the chopped herbs (if using).

4 To keep the sauce warm until you are ready to serve it, set the pan back over the bain-marie – do not allow the water to boil. If it curdles when cold, whisk in a tablespoon of hot water.

SAUCES DERIVED FROM BÉARNAISE ~

Sauce valois ~ Combine the basic béarnaise recipe with a little meat glaze – a strong reduction of a beef-bone broth (see page 74). Use to sauce roast game – venison or wild boar.

Sauce choron ~ Combine the basic béarnaise with 1 tablespoon warmed tomato puree and season with a little lemon juice. Use to sauce grilled fish, poached or soft-boiled eggs, grilled tournedos (fillet of beef), or sautéed noisettes of lamb.

beurre maître d'hôtel

PARSLEY BUTTER

A useful little preparation to have to hand in the back of
fridge, this flavoured butter – literally, head-waiter's
butter – is designed to melt on contact with hot food, providing
an instant sauce for plain-grilled fish, steaks, chops, lamb
cutlets or steamed vegetables. French butters, traditionally
unsalted, are naturally pale rather than golden – a result of the
particular breed of cow, the pastures on which the herds graze,
and an absence of additives. The flavour, too, is distinctive,
since the cream, the raw material of the butter, is allowed to
ripen a little, giving the finished product a distinctive, slightly
soured flavour and helping to preserve it in the absence of salt.
The butters of Normandy, particularly those traded in the town
of Isigny, are the most prized, not least because they melt to a
creamy smoothness.

Serves 12 (sauces 12 portions)

250g (9oz) unsalted French butter, softened juice of 1 lemon
2 tablespoons finely chopped flat-leaf parsley
½ teaspoon salt

1 Beat the softened butter until light and creamy. Beat in the lemon juice little by little. Beat in the parsley and season with a little salt. All this can be done in the food processor.

2 Sandwich the soft butter between 2 sheets of cling film and pat it out to the thickness of a pencil. Leave to cool and harden in the fridge for 1 hour, then either cut it into a dozen little squares with a knife, or cut into the same number of little disks with a scalloped pastry cutter.

3 Store in the fridge for a week or in the freezer for as long as you wish (well, a month or two). In a warm kitchen it will defrost sufficiently in 10 minutes. The food to be sauced should be hot enough to melt the edges of the butter on contact and it should not be dropped into place until just before you serve. Watching the butter melt is part of the pleasure.

OTHER USEFUL BUTTERS ~

Beurre à l'ail ~ (garlic butter) For garlic bread this is prepared by pounding 4 fresh garlic cloves with 1 teaspoon salt and blending the resulting mush thoroughly with 250g (9oz) softened unsalted butter. A milder garlic butter (preferred in the north of France and served as an accompaniment to cold hors d'œuvre) can be made by blanching and softening the garlic cloves in salted water first – 10 minutes at a fast simmer.

Beurre d'anchois ~ (anchovy butter) This is a piquant alternative to a maître-d'hôtel butter – just pop a pat on grilled meats or plain-cooked fish to melt in the heat. The preparation also appears on the hors d'œuvre table – good with a bunch of rosy radishes settled on a bed of cracked ice. To prepare, pound 6–8 anchovy fillets (from a can, drained of their oil) with 250g (9oz) softened unsalted butter.

Beurre de crevettes ~ (prawn butter) This is made by preparing a strong reduction of a broth made with the debris of peeled prawns (shells, heads) with flavouring herbs – parsley stalks, bay leaf, leek tops and peppercorns. Use 2 tablespoons of the reduction to flavour 250g (9oz) softened unsalted butter. You can include the prawn meat if serving the butter as part of a seafood hors d'œuvre or with cold poached salmon or turbot. The same process will produce beurre de crabe or d'homard – crab or lobster butter. Shellfish butters are also used to enrich, lightly thicken and give a shine to seafood sauces: cut the chilled butter into small pieces and whisk it piece by piece into cooking broth. Miraculously, the hot broth and the cold butter form an emulsion. Serve without delay – it won't hold for long.

coulis de tomate

FRESH TOMATO SAUCE

A coulis is a runny puree, a preparation of raw vegetables or fruit which can be used on its own as a sauce or can be added to other sauces as an enhancement.

Serves 4

**1kg (2¼lb) field-ripened tomatoes
juice of 1 lemon
sugar to taste
salt and freshly milled pepper**

1 Pour boiling water over the tomatoes in a bowl to loosen the skins, then peel. Slice the tomatoes in half through the equator. Scoop out the jelly and pips and push through a sieve, discarding the solids and reserving the juice.

2 Put the tomato flesh and juice in the blender or food processor with the lemon juice. Reduce all to a smooth puree. Season with freshly milled pepper, a little salt and a pinch of sugar, more if necessary. Serve as it is over grilled fish. Or stir into a mayonnaise to make a dressing for prawns or fish.

vinaigrette

OIL AND VINEGAR DRESSING

This vinaigrette is used to dress a *salade verte*, green salad, which is served after a main course. The inclusion of non-leaf ingredients turns a green salad into a *salade composée*, a mixed salad, whose proper place is among the hors d'œuvres. Some like to eat it as a mop for the last of the meat-juices, others prefer to eat it with the cheese course or as a palate refresher for dessert.

Makes enough to dress a salad for 4

1 tablespoon wine vinegar
½ teaspoon salt
3 tablespoons olive oil

1 Mix the vinegar and salt first, working with a fork to dissolve the crystals before adding the oil, a medium in which the salt crystals cannot dissolve.

2 Add the oil, blend thoroughly, and toss with the salad leaves, well rinsed and patted dry, just before serving. Finish with a dusting of freshly milled black pepper if you wish – though this is not necessary if the oil has a sufficient degree of pepperiness.

VARIATION ~ To convert the vinaigrette to a sauce rémoulade, start with 1 tablespoon mild mustard – Dijon or Pommery – and work in the vinegar and oil. This is the classic dressing for celeriac salad but is excellent on a green salad, beetroot or potato salad.

FRENCH SALADS ~ An astonishing variety of edible leaves, both cultivated and wild, are available in French markets throughout the year. All are eaten as salads when young and tender, though the same leaves may appear later in the year as cooked vegetables. When designed for a salad, the choice is for texture and flavour – bitter or mild, crisp or soft, sweet or sharp – with a view to complementing the dishes the salad is designed to precede or follow.

If the main course is, say, a robust meat dish, a touch of bitterness is appropriate – frisée (curly-leafed endive), chicory, dandelion (pis-en-lit – a diuretic, as its name implies). If the main course is fish, the leaves chosen should be equally delicate: lamb's lettuce (mâche), young spinach. If the main course is rich and creamy – butter-roast chicken, a creamy fish dish, a quiche or a gratin dauphinois – the choice will be for mustardy leaves such as rocket, watercress or the refreshing sharpness of sorrel.

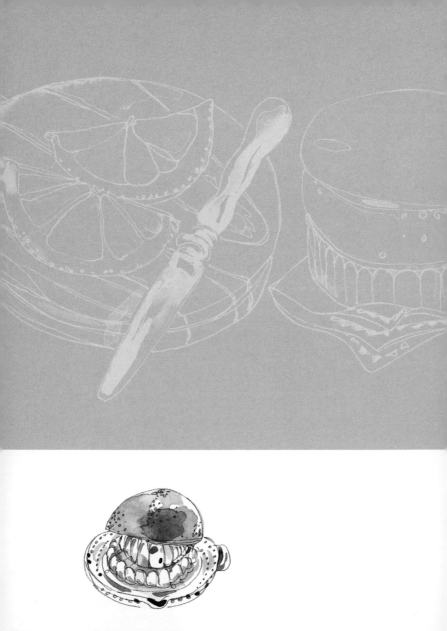

desserts

sirop

STOCK SYRUP

A basic stock syrup, sterile and storable in the larder, can be used to sweeten anything you please without the bother of dissolving sugar crystals. Use to sweeten fruit salads, fruit coulis and berry vinegars. As a soaking syrup for babas, flavour with rum (see page 318).

Makes about 450ml (¾ pint)

500ml (17fl oz) water
500g (1lb 2oz) caster sugar

1 Pour the water into a small saucepan. Add the sugar and dissolve it in the water over a gentle heat.

2 Bring to the boil and simmer for 10 minutes, until reduced by a third. Remove from the heat and leave to cool. Bottle in sterilised jars and seal tightly for storage – no need to keep it in the fridge.

praline

CARAMELISED NUTS

The praline is a flavouring ingredient in its own right,
used in much the same way as chocolate, vanilla or coffee
and kept conveniently to hand in the storecupboard.

Makes 250g (9oz)

250g (9oz) blanched almonds
250g (9oz) caster sugar

1 Line a baking sheet with non-stick baking parchment. Roast
the almonds gently in a dry pan until lightly toasted all over,
stirring to avoid burning – remove as soon as they change colour.

2 Melt the sugar with 1 tablespoon water in a copper pan,
stirring until the crystals have completely dissolved. Bubble
up and cook until the syrup turns pale brown – 4–5 minutes.

3 Add the almonds, stir for 1 minute, and remove from the
heat. Pour on to the prepared baking sheet and leave to cool.

4 Pound the praline in a mortar and store in it a stoppered
glass jar until required.

coulis de framboise

RASPBERRY COULIS

A simple fruit puree sweetened with sugar syrup, this is one of the basic sauces of the French dessert table. It can be used as a foundation for creamy desserts as well as to sauce anything and everything which might benefit from its sharpness and intensity of flavour. Other berries suitable for a coulis are blueberries, blackcurrants and strawberries (for these, add a little lemon juice to bring out the flavour).

Makes 600ml (1 pint)

500g (1lb 2oz) fresh raspberries
250g (9oz) caster sugar
1 tablespoon lemon juice

1 Pick over the raspberries, discarding hulls and any mouldy berries. Transfer to a food processor or liquidiser. Add the sugar and lemon juice, and blitz until you have a smooth puree. Sieve to remove the pips.

SERVING SUGGESTIONS ~ There are various ways of using a coulis de framboise:

- As a sauce for creamy desserts – ice cream, bavarois, cream-stuffed pastries.
- As a flavouring for the dessert itself. For flavouring a hot soufflé, fold with egg yolk and proceed as for soufflé au grand marnier (see page 280). For a mousse, dissolve a little sponged or soaked gelatine in the coulis and fold in whipped cream and firmly whisked egg white. For an ice cream, stir raspberry coulis into its own volume of Crème Anglaise (see page 266) lightened with whipped cream, freeze until almost solid, beat to a foam with an egg white, and freeze again until firm.

NOTE ~ Foods served frozen need more vigorous flavouring than foods to be eaten at room temperature. Sweeten the puree more than you think necessary, and sharpen it up with a squeeze of lemon.

crème pâtissière

CONFECTIONER'S CUSTARD

This is a rich egg custard thickened with cornflour for a smooth finish – older recipes use wheat flour.

Makes about 750ml (1¼ pints)

600ml (1 pint) full-cream milk
short length of vanilla pod
3 egg yolks
75g (3oz) caster sugar
50g (2oz) cornflour
25g (1oz) unsalted butter

1 Add the vanilla pod to the milk and bring to the boil in a heavy-based saucepan. Remove from the heat, lift out the vanilla and scrape the seeds into the milk, then discard the pod.

2 In a roomy bowl, whisk the egg yolks until fluffy. Whisk in the sugar, a tablespoonful at a time, and continue whisking until the mixture is white and light. Sprinkle in the cornflour and whisk until combined.

3 Gradually add the hot milk, whisking until all is blended. Pour the custard back into the pan and bring to the boil, whisking throughout, and boil for 1 minute until smooth and thick. Tip the custard back into the bowl, dot with butter to prevent a skin from forming, and leave to cool.

4 Use to fill pastries, such as choux buns, eclairs, or pancakes; spread in a tart base and top with fresh fruit.

PREPARATIONS DERIVED FROM CRÈME PÂTISSIÈRE ~

Crème au beurre ~ (French butter cream) This is a confectioner's custard made firm enough to set into a layer without support – useful for layering up a sponge-cake, assembling a mille-feuille. Cut 250g (9oz) softened unsalted butter into small pieces and gradually whisk them into the hot crème pâtissière. The custard will thicken as it cools and the butter solidifies.

Crème au chocolat ~ (chocolate cream) Melt 125g (4½oz) dark plain chocolate with the milk when you bring it to the boil with the vanilla, and proceed as above.

Crème au café ~ (coffee cream) Stir a little very strong, very black coffee into the milk.

Crème pralinée ~ (praline cream) Stir in 3–4 tablespoons well-pounded praline (see page 261) when the cream has cooled.

Crème anglaise ~ (pouring-custard) Dilute the recipe with its own volume of single cream plus a little milk, if you like it even runnier.

Ile flottante ~ (floating island) Make a crème anglaise (above) with 6 egg yolks, reserving 4 of the whites. Whisk the reserved whites with 4 tablespoons caster sugar to make a meringue and use 2 tablespoons to form egg-shaped meringues. Poach the meringues gently in simmering water for a few minutes until set. Float these soft meringues, the 'islands', on the custard.

sabayon

WHISKED WINE CUSTARD

A pouring sauce which takes the place of a crème anglaise when serving pastry-based desserts – fruit tarts, feuilletés.

Makes 1.5 litres (2¾ pints)

6 fresh free-range eggs
6 tablespoons caster sugar
about 180ml (6fl oz) white wine

1 Crack the eggs into a bowl which will fit over a saucepan. Whisk the eggs until fluffy. Add the sugar gradually and whisk until white and light – 5 minutes with an electric beater (that is, twice as long as you think). Whisk in the wine.

2 Place the bowl over a panful of boiling water or use a bain-marie – the base should sit clear of the water which should simmer rather than boil. Beat the mixture until it is firm enough to hold the mark of the whisk.

3 Remove from the heat and cool the bottom of the basin in cold water to halt the cooking process. Use to sauce desserts or as the basis for an ice cream flavoured with a fruit liqueur – Cointreau, Grand Marnier, Crème de Cassis.

glace à la vanille

VANILLA ICE CREAM

Nothing is simpler or more delicious than a plain vanilla ice cream – a revelation. Perfect with meringues, as a filling for choux buns, with fresh berries and a crisp langue de chat. For a lighter ice, omit the cream. For a glace au chocolat (chocolate ice cream) melt 125g (4½ oz) dark chocolate into the milk before you remove it from the stove. For a glace au café (coffee ice cream) flavour the milk with instant coffee diluted with a little boiling water, or mix in a tiny cup of strong coffee. For a glace praliné (praline ice cream) fold in 2 tablespoons praline (see page 261) after you fold in the whipped cream. For a glace aux fruits (fruit ice cream) replace the whipped cream with 300ml (½ pint) fresh fruit puree – strawberry, raspberry, blueberry, peach, apricot or banana – or combine the finished mixture with an equal volume of prepared fruit coulis (see page 262).

Makes about 1 litre (1¾ pints)

300ml (½ pint) full-cream milk
½ vanilla pod
4 egg yolks
4 tablespoons caster sugar
300ml (½ pint) double cream

1 Bring the milk and vanilla pod to the boil in a roomy pan, remove from the heat, cover and leave to infuse for 30 minutes in a warm place. Scrape the little sticky seeds from the pod and add them to the milk, discarding the pod.

2 Meanwhile whisk the egg yolks and sugar in a bowl until light and pale. Whisk in the infused milk. Set the bowl over a pan of simmering water and keep the water at a gentle bubble. Stir the custard constantly until it is thick enough to coat the back of a wooden spoon. Remove from the heat, transfer to bowl and leave to cool.

3 Lightly whip the cream and fold it into the custard. Transfer to a container for freezing. When the ice cream is half-frozen, remove from the freezer and beat the mixture thoroughly to break up the ice crystals. Freeze it again until firm.

4 Transfer the ice cream from the freezer to the fridge 30 minutes before serving to let it soften a little.

sorbet aux fraises

STRAWBERRY WATER ICE

The sorbet, as its name suggests, takes its cue from the chilled syrup-flavoured waters much appreciated in Arab lands. At its simplest, a sorbet is nothing more than frozen flavoured water beaten to increase the volume and lighten the texture. The inclusion of either egg white or a dash of some form of distilled liquor – fruit brandy, Calvados, marc – produces a softer consistency since neither substance actually freezes solid. To prepare a sorbet cassis (blackcurrant sorbet), poach 500g (1lb 2oz) blackcurrants in 300ml (½ pint) sugar syrup (see page 260) until the fruit collapses – 4–5 minutes. Allow to cool, sieve or liquidise in a blender. To prepare a sorbet framboise (raspberry sorbet), stir 500g (1lb 2oz) raspberries and 1 tablespoon lemon juice into 450ml (¾ pint) boiling sugar syrup. Allow to cool and push through a sieve or liquidise in a blender. To prepare a sorbet au citron (lemon sorbet), add 150ml (¼ pint) lemon juice to 600ml (1 pint) sugar syrup – taste, add more sugar if the flavour is too bland, or add water if it's too sharp.

Makes about 1 litre (1¾ pints)

500g (1lb 2oz) ripe strawberries, hulled
juice of 1 lemon
300ml (½ pint) sugar syrup (see page 260)
1 egg white

1 Pick over the berries, chop roughly, then mix with the lemon juice and the sugar syrup. Push through a sieve or tip everything into a blender and process to a puree.

2 Freeze the puree in an ice cream maker or transfer it to a metal or plastic container and place in the freezer until just crystallised. Beat thoroughly to break up the ice crystals. Taste and add more lemon juice or extra sugar if the flavour is too subtle – freezing masks sweetness.

3 Whisk the egg white, then whisk it into the sorbet. Beat thoroughly to increase the volume and lighten the texture. Freeze until firm.

petits pots à la crème

VANILLA CREAM CUSTARDS

A simple dessert, this is exquisite with the little fraises de bois
that come into the markets in early spring – the smaller
the berry, the more intense the flavour. They are also heaven
with wild strawberries, sliced peaches, or orange segments
dressed with a splash of Cointreau. To prepare crèmes caramel
(caramel custards), drop a little caramelised sugar into each
ramekin before you pour in the custard. To prepare a caramel,
heat 3 tablespoons caster sugar with a little water until the
sugar crystals melt, bubble up until the sugar browns. Then
swirl a little of the caramel around the base of each ramekin.
The caramel will melt and spread of its own accord, making a
sticky little brown sauce.

Serves 6

2 eggs and 4 egg yolks
600ml (1 pint) single cream
3 tablespoons caster sugar
seeds scraped from a short length of vanilla pod

1 Preheat the oven to 160°C (325°F, gas 3). Prepare a roasting tin with six little ramekins in it.

2 Whisk the whole eggs and the yolks with the cream and sugar – or whizz them up in a food processor. As you whisk or whizz, add the tiny seeds scraped from the vanilla pod.

3 Divide the custard among the ramekins – each should be about half full. Pour enough boiling water into the roasting tin to come half way up the outsides of the ramekins. Cover the baking tray with foil, shiny side down.

4 Bake for 45–50 minutes, without allowing the water to boil again, until the custards are set round the sides but still soft in the centre.

5 Remove the ramekins from the water and leave to cool. Refrigerate for an hour or two – longer if necessary.

petits pots au chocolat

LITTLE CHOCOLATE POTS

O ne of the few desserts the French housewife prepares at home, this is the simplest but most delicious of all chocolate desserts. Neither a mousse nor a custard but something in between, the secret of success lies in the quality of the chocolate and the freshness of the eggs (save the whites to make meringues – see page 290). Perfect with almond tuiles or any crisp, little biscuit. The usual strictures about raw eggs apply.

Serves 4–6

**150g (5oz) best-quality dark chocolate
(at least 70% cocoa solids)
4 tablespoons orange juice, heated to just below boiling
4 eggs, separated
1 teaspoon finely grated orange zest
about 1 tablespoon caster sugar**

1 Break the chocolate in small pieces and place in a bowl set over simmering water. Add the orange juice and stir until melted and perfectly smooth.

2 Remove the bowl from the heat and beat in the egg yolks one by one – they will cook and thicken a little in the residual warmth. Allow to cool to finger temperature.

3 Whisk the egg whites until perfectly stiff. Fold the egg whites into the chocolate with the orange zest, and taste to make sure the mixture is sweet enough: if not, fold in a little caster sugar.

4 Spoon into individual soufflé dishes or, if you have them, special purpose-made chocolate pots. Set them in the fridge for a few hours to firm

MELTING THE CHOCOLATE ~ If the heat is too high, the chocolate will change texture and look grainy – the chocolatière's word is 'seize', an exact description of what happens. To return the chocolate to its liquid state, beat in a little warm clarified butter or oil and beat it until it is smooth again.

VARIATIONS ~ the basic chocolate mixture:
• For petits pots au café, replace the orange juice with the same volume of strong black coffee.
• For petits pots à la cannelle, melt the chocolate with coffee, as above, and stir in a pinch of powdered cinnamon.

crème brulée

*I*n the days when every rural household in dairy country kept a milk-cow, the first spring milkings which became available after the birth of her calf, were as thick and rich as butter. When ladled into a shallow dish, this exceptionally creamy milk set quite solidly enough to be given a caramel-topping without the need to thicken it first with egg yolk. Hence the name – burnt cream. This is a creamy custard topped with caramelised sugar – simple but delicious. Before we all had the benefit of eye-level grills, the sugar topping was melted with a salamander – a red-hot iron heated on the stove.

276

Serves 4

300ml (½ pint) double cream
short length of vanilla pod
1 tablespoon sugar
3 egg yolks

1 Preheat the oven to 170°C (325°F, gas 3). Warm the cream to blood temperature with the vanilla pod. Stir in the sugar to dissolve it. Whisk in the yolks. Take off the froth, remove the vanilla pod, and pour the custard into 4 individual ramekins. Set them in a roasting tin. Pour enough boiling water into the roasting tin to come half way up the outside of the ramekins.

2 Bake for 30–40 minutes, until the custards are set but not hard – they should have just a little give, but not wobble all over the place. Check them during the cooking to make sure they do not scramble. Let the custards cool in the fridge for 8 hours – where they set a bit more.

3 When you are ready to serve, preheat the grill. Sprinkle the surface of the custards with a thin, even layer of brown sugar. Dip your hand in cold water and sprinkle a few drops on the sugar – only enough to dampen it slightly. Pop the ramekins under the very hot grill to caramelise the sugar. If you have a blow-torch in the toolkit, that's a very good way of doing it. Classically delicious.

bavarois aux framboises

RASPBERRY MOUSSE

I n the midst of gloom induced by contemplating modern life,
philosopher-novelist Michel Houellebecq allowed the hero of
Atomised *to find solace in sweet things: "He ordered a
raspberry bavarois and two glasses of kirsch: it was time to
return to simple pleasures".*

Serves 6–8

25g (1 oz) leaf gelatine or 2 sachets powdered gelatine
375g (13oz) caster sugar
juice of 1 lemon
600ml (1 pint) fresh or frozen raspberries
600ml (1 pint) double cream
sweet almond oil or any flavourless oil for brushing mould

1 Both leaf and powdered gelatine need soaking in cold water
before they are added to a recipe. If using leaf gelatine, cover
with cold water and leave until soft – 5 minutes or so – then
squeeze dry. If using powdered gelatine, sprinkle it over
4 tablespoons cold water and leave for 5 minutes without stirring,
until it goes spongy. The gelatine is now ready for use and can be

stirred into a hot liquid without worrying that it will make the mixture lumpy. If you are adding gelatine to a cold liquid, melt the soaked or sponged gelatine gently first, without stirring, in a bowl over hot water.

2 Dissolve 250g (9oz) of the sugar in 150ml (¼ pint) boiling water, stirring until the crystals have dissolved. Warm to just below boiling, then remove from the heat, add the lemon juice and the gelatine and stir until well blended. Allow to cool a little.

3 Save a few of the most perfect raspberries for decorating, then combining the rest with the gelatine mixture. Transfer to a blender and process to a puree, then sieve.

4 Tip the mixture into a bowl and leave it to cool to a soft set – 2–3 hours in the fridge. Choose a single large jelly mould, or pick 12 individual moulds (small tumblers make a pretty shape), and brush with almond oil – cold water will do, but the unmoulded bavarois may not be quite so perfect.

5 Whip the cream with the remaining sugar. Fold into the softly set jelly, turning it over gently with a metal spoon until well blended. Spoon the mixture into the prepared mould(s) and transfer to the fridge for another 2 hours, until set.

6 To unmould, rinse a serving plate with cold water (this will allow you to slide the dessert gently into place if necessary). Run hot water over the outside of the mould, and place the plate on top. Turn the plate and the mould over together and shake to loosen. Remove the mould and finish with the reserved raspberries.

soufflé au grand marnier

SOUFFLÉ *with* ORANGE LIQUEUR

My maternal grandmother, a belle from Baltimore and a friend of Wallis Simpson, employed a real French pastry chef whose speciality this was. I was sixteen before I was allowed to taste it, which was a little unfair since I had been allowed to wield the whisk on the eggs since I was ten. The flavouring can be Cointreau or Curaçao or any other sticky liqueur that takes your fancy. Good with a langue de chat (see page 324), almond tuile or any other crisp little biscuit.

Serves 4

6 eggs plus 3 egg whites
250g (9oz) caster sugar
4 tablespoons Grand Marnier
finely grated zest and juice of 1 orange
½ teaspoon salt
butter and caster sugar for the soufflé mould
icing sugar for dusting

1 Preheat the oven to 200°C (400°F, gas 6). Have ready a souffle mould, 21–22cm (8–9 in) in diameter, well buttered and sprinkled with caster sugar.

2 Separate the eggs, reserving the yolks and adding the whites to the extra 3 whites and set aside. Whisk the yolks in a bowl, adding the sugar spoonful by spoonful, and carry on whisking until the mixture is fluffy and pale.

3 Fold in the Grand Marnier, 2 tablespoons of the orange juice and 1 teaspoon of the zest. Whisk the egg whites with the salt until they hold their shape. Using a metal spoon, fold them into the whisked yolks, turning the mixture gently to blend thoroughly.

4 Spoon the mixture into the soufflé mould – it should be about two-thirds full – and run a knife between the mould and mixture to encourage an even rise. Transfer to the oven and bake for 20 minutes.

5 Open the oven very carefully and check that the top is well risen and crusty – if it is still a little trembly, return it for another 5 minutes (don't bang the oven door as you close it). Dust with icing sugar and serve immediately.

NOTE ~ While the soufflé is baking, make a little orange sauce by simmering 300ml (½ pint) freshly squeezed orange juice and the zest cut into fine match-stick strips with enough sugar – 4 tablespoons – to make a sticky syrup. Finish with a knob of butter chopped into little pieces and a tablespoon or two of whatever liqueur you have used to flavour the soufflé.

crêpes sucrées

S *weet pancakes – crêpes – are rarely eaten on their own but serve as containers for jams or flavoured custards, with which they are stuffed and rolled, or folded in four like a pocket-hankie.*

Serves 4 (about 12 pancakes)

125g (4½oz) plain flour
1 tablespoon vanilla sugar
2 eggs
300ml (½ pint) milk
1 tablespoon brandy or Calvados
butter for greasing the pan

1 Sift the flour into a bowl and mix in the sugar. Make a well in the middle and work in the egg and enough milk to give you a batter with the consistency of single cream. Leave it to develop for an hour or two. Stir in the brandy or Calvados.

2 Heat a small frying pan. Roll a small knob of butter around it. When it foams, pour in enough pancake batter to coat the base of the pan. If you tip in too much, pour the excess back into the bowl immediately.

3 Let the batter set over the heat – when the top surface is dry, flick the pancake over to brown the other side. Flip it out on to a clean cloth. Tuck it up to keep it warm. The first pancake never works properly. Treat it as a test run to tell you if the pan is hot enough and to get the right amount of mixture. Continue until all the batter is used up.

DISHES DERIVED FROM CRÊPES SUCRÉES ~

Crêpes normande ~ Fill the pancakes with apple puree flavoured with Calvados, roll up or fold in four to enclose the filling. Arrange in a gratin dish, sprinkle with sugar and heat in the oven until piping hot and lightly caramelised on top. Serve with the thick slightly soured cream of Normandy.

Crêpes cèvenoles ~ Fill the pancakes with chestnut puree, sweetened, and flavoured with rum. Finish as for crêpes Normande.

Crêpes à la confiture ~ Spread the pancakes with jam and roll up like bolsters. Finish as for crêpes Normande.

galettes bretonnes

T he Bretons make their pancakes with buckwheat, a
primitive grain with a rough texture and a nutty taste
which thrives in harsh conditions. Although a galette can
be made with buckwheat alone, a proportion of wheat-flour
lightens the mix.

Makes a dozen

250g (8 oz) strong white flour
250g (8 oz) buckwheat flour
a pinch of salt
1 level teaspoon baking powder
2 eggs, forked to blend
300ml (½ pint) milk
Goose fat, oil or butter for greasing

TO SERVE
12 tablespoons plum jam
about 100g (4oz) unsalted butter

1 Sieve the flours with the salt and baking powder and then whisk in the rest of the ingredients till you have a smooth cream. Leave for 10 minutes.

2 Heat a griddle or heavy frying pan, grease it lightly with a cloth dipped in goose fat, oil or butter. Test the heat with a drop of the mixture – it should sizzle and set immediately.

3 Pour on enough of the mixture to cover the base of the pan. Cook over a medium heat until the top looks dry. Flip it over and set the other side. Continue till all the mixture is used up. Keep the pancakes warm in a clean cloth while you work.

4 Don't roll the galettes, fold them into quarters and fill with plum jam and a knob of butter. Or roll and shred into noodle-like strips and serve with cream and honey.

NOTE ~ For a savoury version, use as a wrapper for a grilled sausage or a slice of bacon or enclose a raw egg in its folds.

clafoutis aux cerises

CHERRY BATTER PUDDING

A batter which is raised with eggs and nothing else
sometimes bounces up and sometimes doesn't. No matter –
it will be delicious anyway. Any small fruit that can be cooked
in its skin will do – damsons, blueberries, blackberries,
blackcurrants – but if you choose black cherries, the juice bleeds
beautifully into the golden crust. Wonderful with the thick
yellow cream of Normandy. De-stalk, wash and dry the cherries.
Don't stone them – live dangerously.

Serves 4

3 heaped tablespoons plain flour
3 level tablespoons caster sugar, plus extra for dusting
3 eggs, lightly whisked
450ml (¾ pint) milk, warmed
a big knob of butter
¼ teaspoon of vanilla seeds, scraped from the pod,
or a drop of vanilla essence
250g (9oz) black cherries

TO FINISH
Kirsch or dark rum – Negrita gives the right flavour (optional)

1 Preheat the oven to 220°C (425°F, gas 7). Fold the flour and sugar into the whisked eggs. Beat in the warm milk with the vanilla to make a smooth batter.

2 Preheat a baking dish – wide, shallow and about the size of a small roasting tin – and drop in a small knob of butter. Roll the butter around the tin to grease it.

3 Tip in the batter – it'll be sloppy – and sprinkle the cherries over. Dot with butter and bake for 25 minutes, until puffy and well risen.

4 Finish with a good sprinkle of the liquor (if using) and a thick dusting of sugar, and serve without delay, before it subsides.

beignets de pommes

APPLE FRITTERS

The apples considered suitable for cooking are yellow fleshed, sweet and fragrant and are expected to hold their shape in the heat. The choice is usually between pommes reinettes and Golden Delicious – les golden. In apple territory, where beer or cider replace wine as the everyday refreshment, the fritter batter is lightened with beer and flavoured with Calvados or some other white brandy – kirsch, eau de vie de poire or prune – which has the virtue of evaporating as soon as it hits the frying pan, leaving the coating crisp, airy and with a subtle, flowery fragrance.

Serves 4

**4 yellow-fleshed apples
1 tablespoon Calvados or kirsch plus a little extra
a little lemon juice
1 egg
125g (4½oz) plain flour
300ml (½ pint) light beer
oil for deep frying (lard is traditional)
sugar to sprinkle**

1 Peel and core the apples, slice them into rings about 1cm (½in) thick, and reserve (you may if you wish sprinkle the slices with a little Calvados or kirsch). A sprinkling of lemon juice will prevent them from browning.

2 Break the egg into a bowl and whisk to combine the yolk with the white. Sift in the flour. Whisk vigorously to blend, adding the beer gradually until you have a thick cream capable of coating the back of a wooden spoon. Whisk in the Calvados or kirsch.

3 Heat a deep pan of oil for deep frying – don't stint, you need plenty. When a light blue haze rises from the surface – the sign that the oil has reached the right temperature – immediately dip a few slices of apple into the batter and drop them into the fryer. Add three or four at a time – no more, or the temperature will drop and the beignets will be soggy. A frying time of 3 minutes is enough.

4 Lift out the fritters, drain and transfer to kitchen paper to soak up excess oil, then sprinkle with sugar. Continue until all are done.

meringues chantilly

MERINGUES *with* WHIPPED CREAM

A simple recipe which needs nothing more than patience both in the beating and the baking. The secret is the gentleness of the oven, a matter of drying out rather than baking: in high summer, it's possible to cook meringues in the heat of the sun alone. Save the yolks for a custard (see page 264) or to make mayonnaise (see page 163).

∽

Makes 12–14 meringues

4 large egg whites
225g (8oz) caster sugar

TO FINISH
whipped cream

1 Line a baking sheet with non–stick baking parchment. Preheat the oven to 110°C (225°F, gas ¼) or on the coolest setting. Leave the door ajar to keep the temperature as low as 75°C (167°F) if possible. If the oven is too hot, the meringue will weep a sticky residue and it won't set.

2 Everything must be squeaky clean before you begin – the bowl, the whisk, the spoon with which you fold in the sugar. Above all, the egg whites must have no trace of yolk. Whisk the egg whites until light and white.

3 With a metal spoon, fold in half the sugar. Carry on whisking until firm and shiny. Fold in the remaining sugar and whisk until satiny and perfectly firm – the mixture should stay in the bowl if you turn it upside down.

4 Using 2 tablespoons, drop spoonfuls of meringue on to the prepared baking sheet. Bake for 3 hours, until perfectly crisp and dry. The middle should still be a little sticky. Cool and then sandwich the meringues together with whipped cream.

pâtisserie

pâte feuilletée

PUFF PASTRY

Makes about 450g (1lb)

200g (7oz) unsalted butter, chilled
250g (9oz) plain flour
½ teaspoon salt

1 Make the pastry in a very cool place. See that the butter is firm without being hard. Sift the flour with the salt into a roomy bowl. Cut in a third of the butter with a sharp knife until you have a mixture resembling fine breadcrumbs.

2 Mix in about 2 tablespoons water – enough to make a dough that is soft but does not stick to the fingers. Knead lightly. Set the dough aside for 20 minutes, with the rest of the butter beside it so that pastry and butter both reach the same temperature.

3 Roll out the pastry to a thickness of about 5mm (¼in). Dot with small pieces of butter the size of hazelnuts, using about a third of the total quantity. Then fold the pastry into three, like a napkin. Fold again into three, with the folds in the opposite direction. Set aside for 20 minutes.

4 Repeat the process twice more, rolling out the pastry, adding the same amount of butter each time and folding it. Set the pastry aside for 20 minutes after each process. Then leave it for

another 20 minutes before you roll it out and cut it into any shape you please.

5 Bake puff pastry in a hot oven 225°C (430°F, gas 7) for 20–30 minutes, until well risen, crisp and golden.

VOL-AU-VENT CASES ~ For vol-au-vent cases choose two round cutters, one larger than the other. Using the larger of the cutters, cut the dough into neat rounds; with the smaller cutter, press a circle into the middle of each round without cutting through to the base. When the vols-au-vent are baked, the smaller disks can be lifted off to leave a hollow for the filling and making a lid to place on top. Vol-au-vent cases may be filled with a savoury filling, precooked and bound with a creamy sauce.

MILLE-FEUILLE ~ For a sumptuous mille-feuille, roll out the pastry and cut it into three matching rectangles or circles, dust with icing sugar and bake as usual. Allow to cool. Spread one pastry layer with crème pâtissière, top with another pastry layer and spread with strawberry jam and whipped cream. Top with the third layer and finish with a thick dusting of icing sugar. The filling can, of course, be varied as you please.

GALETTE ~ For a galette, roll two circles of pastry and sandwich together with a layer of home-made marzipan – to prepare, make a paste with ground almonds, a little sugar and enough egg-yolk to bind. Dampen the edges and press them together to prevent the marzipan from running out and prick the top to let the steam out. Plain the top with a little milk and egg, then bake as usual till puffed and crisp.

pâte sucrée

SWEET SHORTCRUST PASTRY

Makes about 450g (1lb)

175g (6oz) plain flour
½ teaspoon salt
50g (2oz) icing sugar
100g (4oz) very cold butter
2 egg yolks

1 Sift the flour into a bowl with the salt and sugar. Make a well in the middle and grate in the cold butter. Mix lightly with a knife.

2 Fork the egg yolks with 1 tablespoon water, drop into the middle of the flour mixture and use your fingertips or the knife to gather all into a soft ball – if you need a little more water, sprinkle in the minimum.

3 Using the tips of your fingers (never the palms), knead the dough lightly for a few minutes, just long enough to form a soft ball – do not overwork it or it will oil and toughen. Wrap the dough in cling film or cover with a clean cloth and leave in a cool place for 30 minutes.

4 Roll out the pastry on a floured board with a floured rolling pin – use short firm strokes, pressing rather than stretching – and cut into the required shape.

VARIATION ~ To make plain biscuits, cut out neat rounds with a wine glass or cookie cutter, prick with a fork to stop bubbling, transfer to a baking sheet and bake for 10–12 minutes at 200°C (400°F, gas 6). Cool on the baking sheet for a few minutes to firm up slightly, then transfer to a wire rack to cool completely. The basic quantity makes 24 little biscuits.

pâte à choux

CHOUX PASTRY

Makes about 750g (1lb 10oz)

125g (4½oz) butter
150g (5oz) plain flour
4 large eggs

1 Roughly chop the butter and put it in a heavy saucepan with
300ml (½ pint) water. Bring to the boil and remove from the
heat as soon as the butter has melted.

2 Sift in the flour gradually, beating with a wooden spoon until
smooth – eliminate the visible pockets of flour. Set the pan
back on the heat and beat the mixture for a few minutes until it is
solid enough to leave the sides clean.

3 Remove from the heat, and allow the paste to cool to finger
heat. Beat in the eggs one by one, beating thoroughly
between each addition. At first the paste will seem reluctant to
accept the eggs; as you persist, it becomes easier to work, rather
as a mayonnaise becomes more malleable. At the end, the paste
should be shiny and fairly soft though still firm enough to hold its
shape when dropped from a spoon.

CLASSIC CHOUX PASTRIES ~ The classic choux-pastry recipes are profiteroles (cream-filled choux buns), pets-de-nons (choux-pastry fritters dusted with sugar) and the Burgundian gougère, a ring of choux pastry flavoured and studded with cheese.

Choux buns ~ To prepare choux buns ready for stuffing, lightly butter a couple of baking sheets (not necessary if using non-stick sheets) and preheat the oven to 180°C (350°F, gas 4). Scoop up nuggets of dough using 2 teaspoons and drop them on to the trays, allowing plenty of space between the dollops for expansion.

Bake the buns for 35–40 minutes, until well puffed, brown and firm. As soon as you take them out of the oven, slip a knife into their sides to let out the steam – if you do not do this, the pastry is likely to soften and collapse. If the insides are still a little doughy, scoop out excess dough with the handle of a teaspoon.

Transfer to a wire rack to cool, then stuff with sweetened whipped cream (crème Chantilly), crème pâtissière (see page 264) or home-made vanilla ice cream (see page 268).

Croquembouche ~ The French wedding cake is a tall pyramid of choux buns stuffed with crème pâtissière stuck together with caramelised melted sugar, a creation attributed to the great 19th century chef-pâtissier, Marie-Antoine Carême. When the moment comes for the cake to be shared among the guests, distribution is easy since all the bride has to do is hit the pile with a silver hammer, sending choux buns in all directions.

PASTRY-MAKING TIPS ~

• The cooler you can keep the pastry while you work, the lighter, crisper and crumblier it will be when it comes out of the oven. This is easier to achieve if all your implements – mixing bowls, rolling pin, board – are made of chilly materials. Professional pastry chefs prefer china for the bowl, marble for the board and a tube of unbreakable glass filled with iced water as the rolling pin, though none of these are essential. If at any stage the pastry becomes too warm, it will begin to look oily and acquire a shine, a sign that the shortening has melted and the pastry will be heavy (carry on – it will still taste good even if it is a little tough).

• Shortening is any type of fat – lard, butter, margarine, goose fat – used in combination with flour to make pastry with or without additional liquid in the form of water or egg yolk and/or brandy. If using butter as the shortening, a useful tip is to pop it in the freezer until it hardens, then grate it into the flour for the preliminary mixing. The amount of extra liquid required depends on the amount of water naturally present in the shortening – some butters and 'spreadable' margarines contain an amazing amount of water.

• Egg yolk acts as a binder for a rich pastry – one with a high proportion of shortening (which can make it overly crumbly when baked). If water is used, make sure it is iced – coolness really does make a difference. The replacement of plain water with alcohol – brandy – delivers a light, crumbly pastry since the alcohol evaporates when heat is applied.

• Proportions for a classic English pie-crust are 2:1 flour to shortening; for a very rich French pâte brisee, the proportions can go as high as 1:1, though this is very crumbly indeed unless you include sugar or grated cheese, both of which act as binders after cooking.

- When mixing a pastry, use the tips of your fingers (never your palm, which is far to warm) to work the shortening and the flour together, and lift them up in the air as you mix to incorporate as much air as possible.

- A resting period in a cool place – after the mixing and before the rolling – allows the flour to absorb the liquid and the fat to become firm, ready for rolling.

- When rolling out a pastry, pat it flat with the rolling pin before you start, then use short sharp strokes, pushing away from your body, pressing rather than stretching.

- When lifting and fitting the pastry into a tart tin, fold it over the rolling pin to support it along its length and ease it gently in place without stretching. If it is stretched, the pastry will shrink during the cooking.

- Allow plenty of edge to remain when trimming. When mending any holes (necessary to contain a runny filling) dampen the edges of the hole before patching with a little pastry.

- Do not overfill a pastry case, even if the recipe has landed you with too much filling, and make sure the filling does not come right up to the rim.

tourte aux noix

WALNUT TART

This is a nut tart from the Périgord, where walnuts are traditionally used to fatten the foie-gras goose. You can also make it with unskinned hazelnuts or almonds – a little roughness is essential for the texture.

Serves 6

175g (6oz) butter
225g (8oz) plain flour
50g (2oz) caster sugar
1 egg, forked to blend

FILLING
1 egg white
300ml (½ pint) double cream
125g (4½oz) walnuts, chopped or ground
(not too thoroughly, or the nuts will oil)
75g (3oz) granulated sugar

TO FINISH
6 tablespoons icing sugar
1 tablespoon brandy
8–10 walnut halves

1 Make the pastry first. Using the tips of your fingers, rub the butter into the flour and sugar, and work in enough egg to give a light, firm dough. Cover with cling film and set aside for 30 minutes.

2 Preheat the oven to 180°C (350°F, gas 4). Roll out the dough on a lightly floured board with sharp strokes of the rolling pin and use it to line a 20cm (8in) tart tin, preferably one with a removable base. Ease the pastry gently into the tin without stretching it. Trim leaving a generous rim of pastry – you don't want to lose any of the height.

3 Prick the base and bake the tart case (no need to fuss with beans and foil lining) for 10 minutes, until the surface looks white and dry.

4 Meanwhile, prepare the filling: whisk the egg white until stiff. Half-whip the cream. Mix the cream and egg white with the walnuts and sugar.

5 Remove the tart case from the oven, allow to cool a little, then spread with the filling. Return the tart to the oven and bake for another 20–25 minutes, until the filling is set and the pastry crisp and golden. Leave to cool.

6 Finish with a layer of icing made by mixing the sifted icing sugar with the brandy and enough water to achieve the consistency of double cream. Spread the icing over the tart with a palate knife dipped in hot water. Let it set for an hour or so and then decorate with walnut halves.

croustade de pommes

DOUBLE-CRUSTED APPLE TART

A speciality of south-western France, you'll find this tart on sale in the markets of the Périgord in the winter months, alongside the foie-gras goose. Crisp buttery layers of flaky pastry are used to enclose sliced apples soaked in Armagnac. The making of the pastry is a skill passed from mother to daughter: fine sheets of dough are stretched out on the fists rather than rolled. A technique of Arab origin employed in the making of both filo and the strudel doughs. The method requires that the layers be separated from one another by a brushing of butter. Here, the technique is somewhere in between that used for a flaky pastry and a filo – an egg-dough (much like pasta) is spread with softened butter. You may, if you prefer, replace the pastry dough with sheets of bought filo – six layers of crust each will be sufficient for both top and bottom.

Serves 6

1kg (2¼lb) yellow-fleshed apples
(Reinettes or Golden Delicious)
about 4 tablespoons Armagnac or brandy

PASTRY
350g (12oz) plain flour
½ teaspoon salt
2 eggs, lightly forked together
200g (7oz) butter, softened
25g (1oz) goose fat or pure pork lard, melted
125g (4½oz) sugar
egg yolk and milk to glaze

1 Peel, core and slice the apples. Sprinkle with the Armagnac –
enough to perfume the apples rather than drown them – and
leave for 1–2 hours to absorb the liquor.

2 Meanwhile, make the pastry. You will need about 150ml
(¼ pint) water. Sift the flour and salt into a bowl. Make a well
in the middle and crack in the eggs. Pull the flour into the eggs
with your hands, working gradually from the edges, adding water
as you go, until you have a soft, smooth dough, exactly as if you
were making home-made pasta. Form the dough into a ball, cover
with cling film and set it aside to rest for 30 minutes – long enough
to soften the gluten in the flour and make the dough more elastic.

3 Beat the butter until creamy and reserve. Roll or pat out the
dough to a thickness of 5mm (¼in). Spread with the softened

butter, leaving a rim of a finger's width around the edge. Fold the dough over itself in three – take one edge and fold a third of the dough over the middle, then take the opposite edge and fold the remaining third over the top.

4 Roll the dough out again – you will need to flour it well. Leave it to rest again for 10 minutes. Repeat the operation – folding and rolling – three times. Finally, cut the dough into 2 pieces and roll each out as thin as possible – paper-thin shows real skill. Leave to dry for 1 hour.

5 Preheat the oven to 180°C (350°F, gas 4). Brush both sheets of pastry with melted goose fat or lard. Reserve one sheet and use the other to line a 25cm (10in) tart tin. Trim off the excess and cut it into 3–4 sheets, then place these gently on top of the lining pastry to form layers.

6 Spread the apple slices in the tart, dusting with sugar as you go. Dampen the edges of the pie, and top with rest of the pastry, laid on in layers as before. Trim and neaten the edges, and glaze the top with a little egg yolk and milk, forked together to blend. Cut a little hole in the top for the steam to escape.

7 Bake the tart for 30–40 minutes, until the pastry is crisp and well-browned. As soon as the pie comes out of the oven, sprinkle it with a little more sugar and extra Armagnac shaken from your fingers.

VARIATION ~ For an open (single crust) tarte aux pommes, line a tart tin with sweet pastry, arrange sufficient apple slices to cover the base, laying them in concentric circles. Fork 150ml (¼ pint) single cream with 2 egg yolks and sweeten with a little sugar. Trickle this between the slices and bake as above.

In France's cities and major towns, the pâtisserie, provides the urban housewife with the sugary treats which are served on special occasions – by no means every day. Domestic cooks rarely bake, preferring to leave the sophisticated tarts, cakes and pastries of the French tradition to the experts. Her country cousin, however, expects to order her tarts and cakes in advance from the baker who, in the villages and small towns of rural France, doubles as the pastry-chef. His bakings reflect the seasons.

Winter tarts in my local market town in the Languedoc were filled with a compote of prunes, or topped with a thick layer of sliced apples perfumed with cinnamon, or crammed with a syrupy tangle of nuts and raisins – deliciously crisp and caramelised in the heat of the wood-fired oven.

Whatever his choice, the scent which curled down the street would be sure to attract a queue of eager customers – if you hadn't ordered in advance, you took your chance. Everyone knew what to expect. The arrival of the first strawberries in the market told you there would be strawberry tarts in the baker. When the first white peaches appeared on the stalls, peach tarts – ivory slivers slashed with scarlet laid in concentric circles on a bed of creamy custard – would be sure to appear in the baker's window. At the end of summer there would be little individual tartlets, a mouthful apiece, filled with the dark-skinned hedgerow fruits of autumn – cassis – blackcurrant, mure – blackberry, prune sauvage – sloes. Finally, as autumn drew down, there would be lemon tarts to be warmed through in the oven as a triumphant conclusion to Sunday's midday dinner.

tarte au citron

LEMON TART

These beautiful sharp-flavoured lemon tarts were a winter speciality of my local pâtisserie when I lived in the Languedoc. Tuesday was market day and the scent of citrus oil and warm butter would mingle with that of the blossom on the lemon trees that provided shade for the stall holders.

Serves 8

175g (6oz) plain flour
1 teaspoon salt
50g (2oz) caster sugar
100g (4oz) butter, well chilled
2 egg yolks

FILLING
100g (4oz) unsalted butter, melted
4 lemons
125g (4½oz) caster sugar
5 eggs

1 You will need a 25cm (10in) tart tin, preferably with a removable base. Sift the flour into a bowl with the salt and sugar. Make a well in the middle and grate in the cold butter. Mix lightly with a knife.

2 Beat the egg yolks with 1 tablespoon water and work them into the flour mixture with the tips of your fingers. Gather the mixture into a ball of fairly soft dough. If you need a little more water to make a soft dough, sprinkle in the minimum. Knead lightly and gently for a short time – this is a very rich pastry and liable to oil. Wrap the dough in cling film or cover with a clean cloth and leave in a cool place for 30 minutes.

3 Preheat the oven to 200°C (400°F, gas 6). Flour a board and roll out the pastry dough into a circle to fit the tart tin. Lay the pastry in the tin, easing it into the corners. Line with foil, weight with a handful of dried beans and bake for 12–15 minutes to set the pastry. Remove from the oven and take out the foil and beans. Leave to cool a little.

4 Reduce the oven temperature to 180°C (350°F, gas 4). For the filling, whisk the eggs and sugar together lightly. Grate the zest from 1 lemon and squeeze the juice from all 4 lemons. Fold the zest, juice and butter into the eggs. Immediately pour the filling into the tart case and put it in the oven to bake for 25 minutes, until the pastry is crisp and the filling perfectly set.

tarte aux fraises

STRAWBERRY TART

There can be nothing more deliciously summery than ripe strawberries embedded in a creamy pillow of custard spread on a base of crisp, buttery pastry. It really is worth making your own shortcrust rather than using bought pastry. When making pastry, keep everything very cool – hands, utensils, ingredients – and if possible use a marble slab for rolling. The colder the ingredients, the lighter the pastry, so pop the butter in the freezer first if it's a hot day. Should the custard scramble – perish the thought – tip it straight in the blender with a tablespoon of cold milk and whizz until smooth. Alternative fillings are fresh raspberries, blackcurrants, peach slices, apricot halves or stoned cherries – choose an appropriate jam for the finishing glaze. Always assemble fresh fruit tarts at the last minute to make sure the pastry remains crisp and the fruit plump and bright.

Serves 10–12

675g (1½lb) strawberries

RICH SHORTCRUST PASTRY
175g (6oz) plain flour
pinch of salt
100g (4oz) butter, well chilled
1 tablespoon caster sugar

CRÈME PÂTISSIÈRE
600ml (1 pint) full-cream milk
4 egg yolks
4 tablespoons caster sugar
1 heaped tablespoon flour
50g (2oz) butter
a dash of Cointreau or fruit brandy (optional)

TO FINISH
2–3 tablespoons sieved strawberry or raspberry conserve

1 Pick over the strawberries and set aside. Make the pastry: sift the flour into a cool bowl with the salt. Grate in the cold butter and toss lightly – or use a knife to cut the butter into the flour instead of grating it. Rub the butter in lightly with your fingertips until the mixture looks like fine breadcrumbs. Mix in the sugar.

2 Working with the fingers of one hand only, add 2–3 tablespoons very cold water – just enough water to form a ball. The dough should be firm but not damp, so you may need more or less water – it depends on the weather and the water content of the butter.

3 Transfer the pastry to a lightly floured board or marble slab, pat it with a floured rolling pin to flatten, and roll out to fit a 25cm (10in) tart tin with a removable base – fluted is prettiest. Using the rolling pin as a support, lift the pastry and lay it in the tart tin. Trim the excess, leaving a generous lip to allow for shrinkage. Lay the trimmings around the rim to make a thicker edge (dampen it first). If the tart case tears anywhere, patch it with a scrap of pastry, dampened with a finger. Prick the base with a fork, line with foil and chill for 30 minutes.

4 Preheat the oven to 190°C (375°F, gas 5). Sprinkle a few dried beans or rice on the foil in the tart (not too many – just enough to weight it down). Bake for 15 minutes, remove the foil and beans, and bake for another 10 minutes, until the pastry is crisp and golden.

5 Meanwhile make the crème pâtissière. Put the milk, egg yolks, caster sugar, flour and butter in a blender and process thoroughly – the butter will make the mixture a little lumpy, but no matter. Pour into a heavy-based saucepan and whisk over a gentle heat until thick – do not let the custard boil for more than 1–2 minutes, just enough to cook the flour.

6 Whisk in the Cointreau or fruit brandy, if using, and tip the custard into a cold bowl. Leave to cool – the butter will solidify and help to thicken the custard.

7 To assemble the tart, remove the edge of the tin, but leave the base in place and spread the custard in the cooled tart. Top with the scarlet fruit. Melt the jam or jelly with its own volume of water and use to glaze the fruit.

" *I strongly believe that culinary love is not about having a French Passport, but about what you feel.* "

Albert Roux

tarte tatin

UPSIDE-DOWN APPLE TART

The demoiselles Tatin, two spinster ladies who kept the station hotel in Lamotte-Beuvron near Orleans at the end of the nineteenth century, achieved culinary immortality with the upside-down apple pie which bears their name. For the pastry, I've suggested a lightly sweetened shortcrust – pâte brisée – but feel free to substitute a buttery puff pastry, pâte feuilletée (see page 294). Tarte tatin is lovely with thick crème fraîche or a crème anglaise (see page 266).

Serves 6

250g (9oz) plain flour
1 tablespoon icing sugar
150g (5oz) butter, softened
1 egg

FILLING
1kg (2¼lb) yellow-fleshed apples
(Reinettes or Golden Delicious)
125g (4½oz) unsalted butter
4 tablespoons caster sugar
1 teaspoon ground cinnamon

1 Make the pastry first. Sift the flour with the icing sugar. Chop the softened butter, add to the flour and rub it in lightly with your fingertips until the mixture looks like fine breadcrumbs.

2 Fork up the egg with a little water and a pinch of salt, and work the liquid into the flour and butter lightly until you have a ball of dough – you may need a little more water. Do not overwork the dough. Form it into a ball, cover with cling film and set aside for 30 minutes – or longer – in a cool place.

3 Preheat the oven to 190°C (375°F, gas 5). Prepare the filling. Peel, quarter and slice the apples (not too finely). Spread 1 tablespoon of the butter over the base of a 25cm (10in) square flameproof baking tin, and sprinkle with 2 tablespoons of the sugar. Caramelise this sugar and butter over a high heat – do not let it burn.

4 Layer the apple slices in the hot tin, sprinkling with cinnamon and the remaining sugar, and dotting with scraps of butter.

5 Roll out the pastry to cover the apples comfortably with a generous flap to spare all round. Lay the pastry over the apples and tuck the flap between the apples and the tin to give an edge when the tart is unmoulded.

6 Bake for about 25 minutes, until the pastry is nicely crisped and golden. Wait for 5 minutes before you tip the tart out, bottom side up (inverting it with a platter) so that the pastry ends up underneath.

madeleines

LITTLE BUTTER CAKES

Madeleines are little shell-shaped cakes of the perfect size to hold between finger and thumb. They are just right for dipping in an infusion of lime-blossom or verveine (verbena), or a chilled glass of mint or orange syrup diluted with well-water – the essence, in other words, of a lazy afternoon in the shade of the wisteria terrace in Proustian high summer. For perfection, you need madeleine moulds, a special baking tray indented with shallow shell-shaped cups, though the mixture can just as well be baked in any individual cake or tart tins, though these should be shallow rather than deep.

Makes about 30

butter for greasing the tins
125g (4½oz) unsalted butter, softened
200g (7oz) caster sugar
200g (7oz) plain flour
1 teaspoon baking powder
6 eggs
1 tablespoon orange-blossom water or orange juice

1 Preheat the oven to 200°C (400°F, gas 6) and butter madeleine tins or small shallow patty tins. Beat the butter with the sugar until light and white – use a wooden spoon, electric beater or food processor.

2 Sift the flour with the baking powder and set aside. Crack the eggs one by one into the butter and sugar mixture, beating thoroughly between each addition until well blended. As you add the last couple of eggs you may need to sprinkle in a spoonful of flour to keep the mixture from splitting.

3 Using a metal spoon, fold in the remaining flour and the orange-blossom water or orange juice. Drop teaspoons of the mixture into the buttered madeleine tins.

4 Transfer to the oven and bake for 8–10 minutes, until the cakes have filled the tins completely and are firm, well-risen and browned. Allow to cool a little, then transfer to a rack. Store in an airtight tin when perfectly cool.

babas au rhum

RUM BABAS

This decadent little dessert has been popular in the brasseries of Paris since the days when Toulouse-Lautrec kept company with the demoiselles of Montmartre. While the recipe – buttery little yeast-raised buns drenched in rum-flavoured syrup – is of Polish origin, it speaks to the French soul of the days of Empire. Rum is produced in the French West Indies, the birthplace of Napolean's Empress Josephine.

Makes 12 babas

2 tablespoons raisins
4 tablespoons rum
350g (12 oz) strong white flour
½ teaspoon salt
25g (1oz) fresh yeast/12g (½oz) dried yeast/1 packet easy-blend yeast
150g (¼ pint) milk, warmed
2 tablespoons sugar
50g (2oz) unsalted butter, melted, plus extra for greasing tins
2 eggs

TO FINISH
1 litre (2 pints) sugar syrup (see page 260)
150ml (¼ pint) dark rum
crème fraîche

1 Put the raisins to soak and swell in the rum for an hour or so.

2 Sift the flour and salt into a warm bowl. If using fresh yeast, blend it to a liquid in a cupful of the warm milk, make a well in the flour, pour in the yeasted milk, sprinkle with a handful of the flour, then set aside for 15 minutes in a warm place for the yeast to begin to work. If using dried yeast, sprinkle it over a cupful of milk and leave to dissolve for a few minutes, before stirring it and pouring with the flour as for fresh yeast. If using easy-bake yeast, mix it into the flour – no need for sponge-setting.

3 Add the sugar and the rest of the milk (or all the milk, if using easy-bake yeast). Work the wet ingredients into the dry to make a soft, smooth dough, leaving any unabsorbed flour loose. Work in the melted butter and the eggs, taking up the unabsorbed flour as you work: persist until all is absorbed, when the dough will be soft and sloppy. Work in the raisins and their soaking rum.

4 Brush 12 individual moulds with melted butter. Divide the dough between the moulds. Set to rise in a warm place for 1–2 hours, until the dough has risen to the top of the moulds.

5 Preheat the oven to 200°C (400°F, gas 6). Bake the babas for 15–20 minutes, until well-risen, brown and firm to the finger. Transfer to a rack to cool completely.

6 Bring the sugar syrup to the boil in a large saucepan. Place the rack holding the babas over a plate to catch drippings of syrup. Drop the babas into the syrup a few at a time, then wait until no more bubbles rise before you remove them with a draining spoon. Transfer the babas back to the rack.

7 Allow to cool a little, then trickle with the rum. Spoon the drippings over the babas as they cool. Serve with crème fraîche.

NOTES ~

• If using easy blend dried yeast, mix it with the flour and use milk that is hand-hot rather than lukewarm, mixing in the whole quantity in one go. No need to set the sponge.

• For an instant version of the babas, use ready made brioches and add the raisins to the soaking syrup instead of baking them in the dough.

It was in France that I first learned about food. And that even the selection of a perfect pear, a ripe piece of Brie, the freshest butter, the highest quality cream were as important as how the dish you were going to be served was actually cooked.

Robert Carrier

reine de saba

ALMOND AND CHOCOLATE CAKE

L ight, buttery and moist, this dark-crumbed cake – queen of Sheba – is flavoured with rum imported from the sugar plantations of French West Indies. France's former colonies are actually overseas departments with the right to send representatives to parliament in Paris. The cake is good with vanilla ice cream and wild strawberries.

butter and flour for greasing and dusting
225g (7oz) dark bitter chocolate
1 tablespoon golden or dark rum, preferably St. James's
150g (5oz) butter
150g (5oz) caster sugar
5 eggs, separated
100g (4oz) ground almonds

1 Preheat the oven to 180°C (350°F, gas 4). Butter an 18cm (7in) square cake tin and dust with flour – if using a round tin, choose one of 20cm (8in) diameter. The cake will be easier to remove if you line the base with non-stick baking parchment.

2 Melt the chocolate with the rum, butter and sugar in a bowl set over a pan of simmering water. Remove from the heat and allow to cool a little.

3 Meanwhile, whisk the egg whites until they hold soft peaks. Beat the egg yolks into the still-runny chocolate. Mix in the ground almonds. Then fold in the whisked whites, adding only a little at first so that the mixture lightens and can accept the rest.

4 Spread the mixture in the prepared tin. Bake for 40–50 minutes, until well risen and firm to the finger. Leave to cool before removing from the tin. If the cake cracks on top, that is part of its charm – fix it with a sprinkle of icing sugar.

langues de chat

FINGER COOKIES

*L*iterally, cats' tongues, these are crisp little biscuits for eating with creamy desserts or ice creams, or just for dipping into a chilled glass of Sauternes or any of France's cellarful of delicious sweet wines. Good too, with one of the aperitifs French housewives keep on the shelf for special occasions: home-made vin d'orange, one of the herb-flavoured vermouths – Noilly or Chambéry – or a drop of cassis diluted with champagne.

Makes about 24 biscuits

butter for greasing and flour for dusting
100g (4oz) unsalted butter, softened
100g (4oz) caster sugar
a knife tip of vanilla seeds or ¼ teaspoon real vanilla essence
2 eggs
100g (4oz) plain flour

1 Preheat the oven to 230°C (450°F, gas 8). Butter a couple of baking sheets and dust with a little flour. Beat the softened butter with the sugar until light and white, adding the vanilla – use a wooden spoon or a food processor.

2 Beat in the eggs, one at a time. Fold in the flour with a metal spoon, turning the mixture over to blend the ingredients. Spoon the mixture into a piping bag fitted with a plain round nozzle and pipe fingers of mixture about 5cm (2in) long, leaving plenty of room between each to allow for spreading.

3 Bake for 5–6 minutes, until the edges have browned and the middles are firm and golden. Remove and transfer carefully to a baking rack to crisp and cool. Store in an airtight container when cold.

the french storecupboard

EVERYDAY CHARCUTERIE

You'll find plenty of regional variety in the charcuterie, the cured-pork shop which provides the French housewife with her basic hors d'œuvres as well as other little delicacies which need minimum culinary attention. No meal however modest or grand – from presidential banquet to school dinner – can be considered complete without its little appetiser, its palate-awakener – a sliver of saucisson, a scrap of jambon cru.

Jambon cru (de Bayonne or de campagne – country ham): salt-cured air-dried ham eaten raw, a light smoking makes it different from Italy's prosciutto and Spain's serrano. Usually served with a little pat of unsalted butter.

Saucisson sec: the French version of Italian salami: salt-cured air-dried all-meat sausage designed to be sliced and eaten raw. Individual appearance and flavour depends on the shape and size of the intestine into which the meat is stuffed, the proportion of fat to meat and the spices and herbs used to season the mix.

Cervelas: a short, thick frankfurter-like boiling-sausage which can also be grilled – good wrapped in a galette bretonne (see page 284), a pancake made with buckwheat flour.

Saucisse de Toulouse: an all-meat pork sausage for frying or grilling. Uncured as well as cured French sausages never contain rusk and are usually spiced rather than flavoured with herbs.

Boudin noir: blood-sausage or black pudding, precooked and finished by grilling or frying; delicious fried in butter with apples.

Boudin blanc: white pudding, a delicate poaching-sausage (though it can also be grilled) made with white meat – pork or chicken – pounded smooth with pork-fat, eggs and cream but no blood. Exquisite with pommes de terre mousselines (see page 94) – fluffy mashed potato.

STORECUPBOARD FISH

Anchois en conserve: In Provence, anchovies, cheap and plentiful in Mediterranean waters, are eaten fresh as well as preserved in salt, the form in which, along with garlic and olive oil, they define the cooking of Provence. While tinned is the form in which they're most widely recognised – filleted, de-salted and preserved under oil – in Provence they're sold direct from the barrel, when they'll need de-salting and de-whiskering – to prepare, brush off the salt-grains and soak in a little milk, then remove the hairy little bones by running your thumb down the spine. To prepare as an anchoïade – dipping sauce for raw vegetables – crush 3–4 anchovy fillets and a sliver or two of garlic into 150ml warm olive oil. When added to a fish-soup or sauce, they melt into the background, subtly heightening the flavour. Quality counts. When serving them as an hors d'œuvre, leave them in the tin with the top rolled down and the label proudly displayed so that all may admire your choice.

Morue: salt-cod, bacalhau, was for many centuries the fast-day food of Roman Catholic inhabitants of the shores of the Mediterranean – a curious situation since the fish itself is only found in the Atlantic. The trade was particularly valuable during the Middle Ages, a time when more than half the year was fasting – meatless days included Wednesdays as well as Fridays, the Eves of all saints days and the forty days preceeding Christmas as well as the Lenten fast. In response to what was intended as deprivation, the resourceful cooks of France, unwilling to eat something which didn't taste good, invented dishes so delicious they're eaten to this day. In French markets around Christmas time, when salt-cod is the traditional dish of the fasting supper which preceeds the feast itself, you can buy your morue ready-soaked. To prepare salt-cod from scratch, choose a piece of middle-cut, pale but not too white (a sign of artificial bleaching), with no trace of pink. Soak it in several changes of water for 36–48 hours till it rehydrates and softens. Cover with fresh water and cook in gently simmering water – don't allow it to boil – for 15–20 minutes, until tender. It can now be prepared as if it were fresh fish: in Provence they like it sauced with tomato, olives, onion and olive oil. In the Rouergue, where nut oils replace the olive oil of the south, they like it beaten into mashed potatoes with walnut oil.

OILS AND COOKING FATS

It is possible to divide the cooking of France into three broad bands according to the inhabitant's preference for cooking with olive oil, goose fat or butter. The inhabitants of the southern regions – Provence and the eastern Languedoc where olive trees thrive – cook with olive oil. For la France Profonde – the central heartland from the Pyranees through the Massif Centrale – the natural choice is goose fat. For the northerners – the inhabitants of Normandy, Brittany, the territories bordering Germany and Belgium, as well as the rich farmlands of the valley of the Loire – the choice is butter. In those areas – particularly Berry – where olive trees cannot thrive and the taste for butter or goose fat is not strongly developed, nut-oils, particularly walnut, replace the olive oil. Although no longer so sharply defined, the distinctions apply to this day.

HERBS IN COMMON USE

Tarragon, the quintessentially French herb, is irreplaceable in butter, cream and wine sauces and has a particular affinity with white meats – chicken and veal, the specialities of the rich farmlands. Rosemary, thyme, savory and several other localised members of thyme family are the flavouring herbs of Provence; these, when grown in harsh conditions on Mediterranean hillsides, lose none of their pungency or even their weight when dried, the form in which they're most fragrant (don't bother with the soft-leaved stuff sold 'fresh' in cellophane packets). Along with marjoram and bay, they have an affinity with pork, beef and game. The Provençale herb-jar includes orange zest – finely-pared and de-hydrated to intensify the flavour – for adding to slow-cooked stews. Central France likes the milder mixes of mustard including those of Dijon and Bordeaux, while northern France has a taste for chives.

In addition to herbs, French storecupboards are usually stocked with a jar or two of dried fungi, a seasonal treat in a form available throughout the year. Only a handful of the wild-gathered fungi which are eaten fresh are suitable for dehydration: of the autumn mushrooms, chanterelles and cèpes are suitable; the best, however, is the morel, a spring mushroom which, though excellent fresh, is even better when dried.

As for the truffle-family, the black or Périgord truffle (also found in considerable quantity in Upper Provence) is sold *en conserve*, tinned or jarred, but it's not a patch on the real thing. And don't bother with the truffle-oil, either – something unrecognisable happens to the flavour, even if it's not a chemical copy. If you have reason to wish to preserve a truffle, buy your own, mash it up with butter and pop it in the freezer.

useful conversion charts

Use this basic guide for converting measurements from metric and imperial to cup measures. Volumes are standard. Weight can vary according to the density of the ingredients, so the basic ingredients should be used as a rough guide.

USING CUP AND SPOON MEASURES	
All cup and spoon measures should be level (unless otherwise stated).	
¼ teaspoon	1.25ml
½ teaspoon	2.5ml
1 teaspoon	5ml
1 tablespoon	15ml

LIQUID MEASURES		
Cup	**Metric**	**Imperial**
¼ cup	60ml	2fl oz
1 cup	250ml	8fl oz
1¼ cups	300ml	½ pint
1½ cups	350ml	12fl oz
1¾ cups	400ml	14fl oz
2 cups	475ml	16fl oz
2½ cups	600ml	1 pint
3 cups	750ml	1¼ pints
4 cups	1 litre	1¾ pints

WEIGHTS			
Metric	**Imperial**	**Metric**	**Imperial**
100g	¼lb	500g	1lb 2oz
175g	6oz	575g	1¼lb
225g	½lb	675g	1½lb
350g	12oz	800g	1¾lb
450g	1lb	1kg	2¼lb

OVEN TEMPERATURES

°C	°F	Gas
110	225	¼
120	250	½
140	275	1
150	300	2
160	325	3
180	350	4
190	375	5
200	400	6
220	425	7
230	450	8
250	475	9

BASIC INGREDIENTS

Cup and Weight Equivalents

Bread crumbs, dry	1 cup = 65g / 2½oz
Bread crumbs, fresh	1 cup = 50g / 2oz
Butter	1 cup = 225g / 8oz 2 tablespoons = 50g / 2oz
Cheese, grated Cheddar	1 cup = 100g / 4oz
Confectioner's sugar	1 cup = 100g / 4oz
Cornstarch	1 cup = 225g / 8oz
Couscous	1 cup = 175g / 6oz
Cream cheese, ricotta	1 cup = 225g / 8oz
Flour	1 cup = 100g / 4oz
Honey	1 cup = 225g / 8oz
Parmesan cheese, grated	1 cup = 75g / 3oz
Peas, frozen	1 cup = 100g / 4oz
Rice, long grain types	1 cup = 200g / 7oz
Sugar, granulated or superfine	1 cup (generous) = 225g / 8oz 1 cup (scant) = 200g / 7oz

INDEX

Entries in *italics* refer to recipe names

A

aligot 98–9
almonds
  praline 261
  reine de saba 322–3
anchovies
  beurre d'anchois 254
  salade niçoise 43
apples
  beignets de pommes
    288–9
  crêpes Normande 283
  croustade de pommes
    304–6
  pintade farcie aux
    pommes 166–8
  tarte tatin 314–15
artichokes
  artichauts à la
    barigoule 62–4
  preparing 64, 65
  tian de blea 120–1
  topinambours à la
    provençale 60–1
asparagus
  asperges à la
    vinaigrette 50–1
aubergines
  ratatouille 46–7
  tian de blea 120–1

B

babas au rhum 318–20
bacon *see* ham and bacon
bavarois aux framboises
  278–9
beef
  bœuf bourguignon
    204–6

consommé 74–7
daube de bœuf 202–3
entrecôte bordelaise
  212–13
entrecôte vigneron
  210–22
pot-au-feu 200–1
steak au poivre 208–9
beef marrow, preparing
  213
beignets de pommes
  288–9
beurre blanc 247
beurre d'ail 254
beurre d'anchois 254
beurre de crevettes 254
beurre maître d'hôtel
  252–3
biscuits
  langues de chat 324–5
  pate sucrée 297
blanquette de veau 220–2
bœuf bourguignon
  204–6
bouillabaisse 140–5
brains 226
  cervelles au beurre
    noir 232–3
brandade de morue
  18–19
butters
  beurre d'ail 254
  beurre d'anchois 254
  beurre de crevettes
    254
  beurre maitre d'hotel
    252–3

C

cabbage
  choucroute 225
  cailles aux raisins
    196–7

cakes
  babas au rhum 318–20
  madeleines 316–17
  reine de saba 322–3
caneton à la bigarade
  169–71
carrots
  carottes vichy 106–7
casseroles
  cassolette d'escargots
    32–3
  cassoulet de
    castelnaudary 178–81
  garbure béarnais 174–6
celeriac
  celeri-rave en
    rémoulade 48–9
cèpes à la bordelaise
  52–3
cervelles au beurre noir
  232–3
champignons à la
  grecque 54–5
chards
  tian de blea 120–1
chaud-froid de poulet
  162–5
cheese
  aligot 98–9
  croque monsieur 68–9
  salade de fromage de
    chèvre chaud 70–1
  soufflé au fromage
    66–7
cherries
  clafoutis aux cerises
    286–7
chicken
  chaud-froid de poulet
    162–5
  coq au vin 158–9
  poulet au beurre 152–4
  poulet au riz 155–7

332